KNITTING AND DESIGN
FOR MOHAIR

ANGELA FFRENCH

KNITTING AND DESIGN
FOR MOHAIR

B.T. BATSFORD LTD
LONDON

ISBN 0 7134 5421 0

Typeset by Servis Filmsetting Ltd, Manchester
and printed in Great Britain by

Anchor Brendon Ltd
Tiptree, Essex

for the publishers
B.T. Batsford Ltd
4 Fitzhardinge Street
London WIH OAH

ACKNOWLEDGEMENTS

Eileen French for working her fingers to the bone.
Betty Chainey for her comments and perfect knitting.
Duncan Annand and Jeremy Mustoe of Annand and Mustoe Architects, Cambridge, for use of the photocopier.
Tom Sharpe for coming to the rescue with a camera when my shutter jammed.
Elisabeth Hohler for constant encouragement, often into the small hours.
Robin Thompson of Houston/Bergström, Cambridge, for his time and enthusiasm.

The models: Clara, Cristina, Eddie, Eileen, Elisabeth, Janine, Jean, Kate, Mayayo, Rosemary, Ruth, Soraya, Vicky and Vikki.

Marian Schröder and the John Lewis Partnership for such generous help with yarns.
W.H. Lister and Lister Handknitting.
Winifred Muir and Pingouin.
William Letima and Lesotho Handspun Mohair.
Ron Irons and Patons and Baldwins, and the many companies worldwide who sent samples and information and encouragement.

And mostly to Mike for his support, advice, criticism, and endless patience and who together with Kerstyn and Æthan put up with fluff in the soup for so long.

CONTENTS

INTRODUCTION

Mohair is rather special. For centuries it has been chosen for its luxurious appearance, its thistle-down softness and its durability. But there is another quality possessed by mohair which until now has been overlooked.

When knitting with other yarns, such as wool, silk, cotton, and linen, the size of a garment is controlled by the number of stitches and the number of rows. With mohair this is not so important. The fibrous nature of the yarn enables a sweater's size to be regulated by the needle size: big needles make a big sweater; small needles make a small sweater. 7 mm needles will produce a looser fabric than 4 mm needles, but the forgiving nature of mohair fills the spaces between the stitches and the effect will be just as good. The beauty of this technique is that once a pattern has been designed the only adjustment that need be made is to the size of the needles.

There are so many stunning mohair yarns on the market that with a little thought and guidance it is possible to create your own beautiful and unique garment using this simple technique.

Mohair is the fleece of the Angora goat, a gentle animal whose origin remains a mystery. The Buddhist monks in the Himalaya say it may be a cousin to their little white goats with delicate spiral horns and long silvery fleeces which were sent by the God Buddha from Heaven. Perhaps it strayed or was driven from Tibet through Persia and along the Caspian into Asia Minor. Moses may have known it, because he was commanded to 'make curtains of goats' hair to be a covering upon the Tabernacle' (Exodus 26:7). But the earliest factual statement on the Angora goat did not appear until 1554 when a pair of goats was sent to the Holy Roman Emperor, Charles V.

Until the sixteenth century the Angora goat was jealously guarded by its Turkish masters, the word mohair being a corruption of the Turkish word 'mukhyar', which means 'the best or selected fleece'. Then a Dutchman came across it and recognized the exceptional quality of the fleece.

At this time in Ankara, the spinning of mohair was done only by women for their families. Outside interest in the fibre grew until demand exceeded supply, so that eventually the Sultan of Turkey forbade the export of unprocessed mohair. In an attempt to meet the growing demand, the Turks crossed the Angora goat with the native Kurdish goat. Unfortunately, the quality of the fleece declined, and the Angora goat ran the risk of extinction.

In 1838, under pressure from England, the export ban was lifted and mohair became more widely known throughout Europe, although only in the form of spun yarn. Many attempts were made to export the goats themselves but failed, mainly because of the delicate nature of the animal. The Angora goat thrives in a warm, dry climate. The earliest successes seem to have been in Spain and France in 1765.

South Africa received its first shipment of twelve bucks and one doe in 1839. On their arrival, however, it was discovered that the twelve bucks had been deprived of their reproductive powers. By chance, the single doe had given birth to a male kid during the journey, and when this kid was crossed with the local goats it produced a hardier animal and better meat – the quality of the hair was not considered important in South Africa at the time.

(courtesy of the International Mohair Association)

It seems that the Angora goat found its way into the United States by accident. A Dr J.B. Davis of Columbia was invited by the Sultan of Turkey to experiment in the production of cotton. When he returned home he took with him nine choice goats, two bucks and seven does. These were mistakenly imported as Cashmeres, and their true identity was not discovered until 1853 when three of the goats came into the hands of Richard Peters of Atlanta, a well-informed breeder of livestock. Publicity about the animals grew and in 1860 one goat fetched $1,500 while another was sold for its weight in silver.

In 1853 a small herd of Angoras was imported to New South Wales from Turkey. By 1901 more than 1,000 goats were being reared at Peak Station near Lake Eyre in South Australia. However, interest in the Angora goat diminished in the 1920s and 1930s, and while a gradual comeback took place in the 1950s and 1960s, real interest has only revived over the last ten to fifteen years.

There are about 6 250 000 Angora goats in the world, mainly in Argentina, Australia, Lesotho, South Africa, Texas and Turkey. In South Africa and Texas the first two shearing are sold as 'kid mohair', the finest quality which realizes the highest price. Next come the young goats and then the adult Angoras, which produce excellent mohair. Each animal provides on average two kilos of hair when shorn, but the total output of mohair is still only one quarter of one per cent of all natural fibres.

In Lesotho the yarn is spun by hand. It takes a woman in the mountainous highlands of Lesotho a day's work to spin 500 g of mohair and the slight irregularity in the yarn she produces creates a rich, individual texture.

A single hair is shaped rather like a bamboo pole, making it slippery and difficult to handle. For this reason the fleece has to be sorted, washed, combed, spun and woven by skilled craftsmen. To regain its natural resilience, the fibre is rested at intervals – the more time taken in processing mohair, the better the final product. It knits up quickly and is soft and silky yet tough and warm, and springs back into shape at each wearing.

1

COMPOSING
A GARMENT

Knitting and Design for Mohair is for knitters and non-knitters. It is written to encourage you to design your own masterpieces and if you can't knit your design you may have a kindly relation who will.

Normally, a plain sweater pattern is quite straightforward. There are only three considerations: the shape of the garment, the size of the garment and the gauge of the yarn. However, the mathematics of working out all those rows and stitches puts many people off.

To simplify this, *Knitting and Design for Mohair* is arranged to cut out the mathematics. All you have to do is choose:

- a body
- an appropriate sleeve
- cuffs
- a collar
- a welt
- accessories

– and you've composed a garment.

> **HANDY TIP**
> To stop the filaments of mohair flying, store the yarn in the fridge until needed.

HOW TO READ THE PATTERNS

Each pattern comes as a squared paper grid with each stitch represented by a square. Basic welts are already added to the grids, but these can be altered if your design includes a special type of welt. If you haven't read a pattern like this before, there are also written instructions, but once you get the hang of reading the grids, you'll see how simple they are to follow.

You will notice that the welts have fewer stitches than the bodies of the garments. This draws the welt in and gives a snugger fit. However, when you come to this point in the pattern remember to increase the extra number of stitches evenly across the row. This also applies to most of the cuffs. Remember, too, that all the welts, collars and cuffs are worked on needles two sizes smaller than those used for the body.

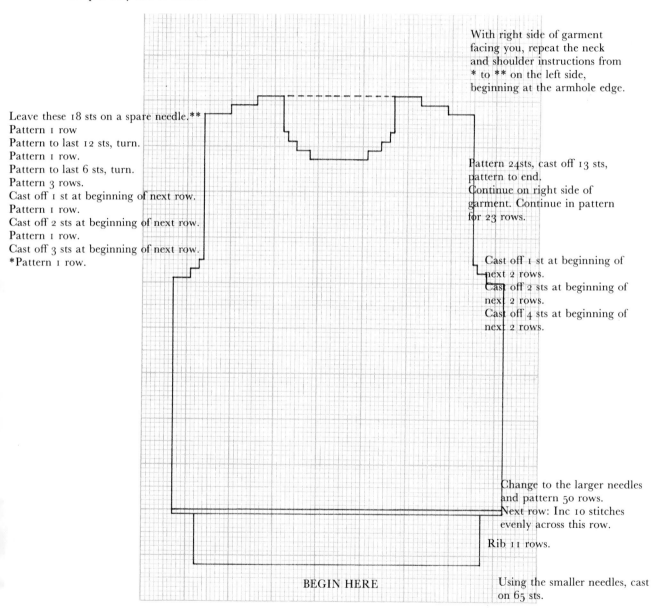

With right side of garment facing you, repeat the neck and shoulder instructions from * to ** on the left side, beginning at the armhole edge.

Leave these 18 sts on a spare needle.**
Pattern 1 row
Pattern to last 12 sts, turn.
Pattern 1 row.
Pattern to last 6 sts, turn.
Pattern 3 rows.
Cast off 1 st at beginning of next row.
Pattern 1 row.
Cast off 2 sts at beginning of next row.
Pattern 1 row.
Cast off 3 sts at beginning of next row.
*Pattern 1 row.

Pattern 24 sts, cast off 13 sts, pattern to end.
Continue on right side of garment. Continue in pattern for 23 rows.

Cast off 1 st at beginning of next 2 rows.
Cast off 2 sts at beginning of next 2 rows.
Cast off 4 sts at beginning of next 2 rows.

Change to the larger needles and pattern 50 rows.
Next row: Inc 10 stitches evenly across this row.

Rib 11 rows.

BEGIN HERE

Using the smaller needles, cast on 65 sts.

14

Unless a separate back pattern is given, the backs are the same as the front but without the neck shaping. The dotted line at the neck edge of the round neck jumper shows where the pattern ends.

Making a cardigan from the round-neck or V-neck patterns is very easy. Draw a line down the centre front of the pattern and then work the two halves separately. These patterns will give you a shorter cardigan than the 'Crossover jacket' or the 'One-piece jacket' (pages 26 and 27).

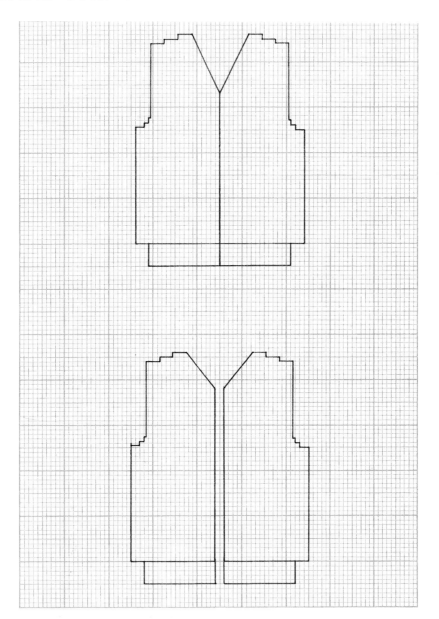

Don't forget the collars and cuffs. There are many ways of brightening up a plain sweater. Do you want a simple rib, a two-tone rib or a fancy rib? Would you like to add tassles or beads? Are the cuffs going to be a regular length, or would you prefer them to be longer, shorter, or not at all? Look through chapters 2 and 3 and select the pieces you need to make up your garment. Chapter 4 should give you some ideas. See how the basic body shapes can be varied with collars and cuffs or by altering the length or using a heavier yarn. Try to draw it, however simply, to get your ideas clear. (You don't have to be a great artist – square shapes are fine for getting down your ideas.)

Make a note of the selected parts:

- round neck body
- shaped sleeve
- cabled cuffs
- cabled collar
- 2 × 2 rib welt
- patch pockets

– and you've got your pattern.

Make sure, however, that you read through the instructions for all the pieces before you begin, so that you knit them in a sensible order.

Now you can decide if you want your garment to be plain or patterned. Would you like Fair Isle patterning, a Scandinavian design, a picture sweater, or would you like to use a variety of stitch patterns? Chapter 6 provides basic rules and useful hints for designing in colour; chapter 7 is a directory of Fair Isle and Scandinavian designs; and chapter 8 is a directory of stitch patterns. Plan the whole sweater on graph paper and then it's time for:

HANDY TIP

To make a firmer, more elastic cuff or welt, work a strand of 4 ply wool or elastic thread together with the mohair. At the end of the cuff or welt, break off the wool or elastic and continue using only mohair.

CHOOSING THE YARN

Yarns containing mohair have a special quality. The long fibres of the mohair fluff out and fill the spaces between the stitches. This means that it is possible to change the size of a garment simply by changing the size of the needles. Fat needles will produce a bigger piece of knitting than thin needles. Now you can make sweaters for all the family using one pattern – the same number of stitches and rows will produce a wide selection of sizes, depending on the needles you use.

Choose yarn of about the same thickness as double knitting wool. If it's much thinner the effect will be too 'holey', and if it's thicker, too matted. However, thicker yarns, bouclés and tweedy mixes, are excellent for big garments, and thin yarns can be used for making smaller garments. (I even made a cardigan for a newly born niece using the dolman pattern, an ultra-fine Italian yarn and 3 mm needles.) You can mix yarns successfully, too – different weights and mixtures add textural interest.

Mohair yarns are available all over the world. Some contain as little as 15 per cent while others are made from pure mohair. There are random-coloured yarns, heather mixes, and yarns that shout their colour at you. There are bouclés and tweeds and soft silk mixes. Some yarns are mixed with metallic threads, and one with a strand of clear film that makes the mohair sparkle; another has the mohair spun at random into a viscose thread.

The yarns in the table have all been tested and can be used with this system. They are arranged in order of weight, the finer yarns at the top of the list being more suitable for smaller garments, and the heavier yarns for large designs.

ESTIMATING QUANTITIES

This can be tricky, as yarns are generally sold by weight and not by length. As a result, 25 g of thick bouclé yarn will be much shorter than 25 g of a fine, pure mohair. Metal threads, silk, acrylic and cotton yarns all affect the weight and therefore the length (per 10 g) of the yarn.

If the yarn you'd like to use doesn't appear in the table on page 19, look at the label. Some yarns have a yardage guide which will help you work out how much you'll need.

Then turn to chapter 9 and see if there's a sweater or jacket in a similar style or yarn to the one you've designed. Is it bouclé or plain? Is there a metallic thread in the yarn? Are you designing a Fair Isle sweater using five or six colours? The example sweaters give yardage as well as weight quantities. How much yarn was needed for the example sweater?

Plain sweaters need to be made from yarn from a single dye batch, or slight variations in colour may appear in the finished garment. It's always safer to overestimate. Multi-coloured Fair Isle or picture sweaters present no problem, since colours spread into each other and changes in dye lots will never be noticed.

Failing all this, ask the sales assistant. She knows by experience and she's handling new yarns all the time. If you overestimate she'll probably be happy to take back the excess yarn – *but* check the time limit on returns and exchanges, and note this on the receipt, which you're going to keep in your knitting bag! If the assistant is no help, go to another shop.

NOTE: Weights of yarns in the text are given in grams, but a gram/ounce conversion chart appears on page 162.

WHICH NEEDLES SHOULD I USE?

This depends on two things:

- the size of the garment
- gauge

Gauge is the most important factor in creating the correct size of sweater. It means the number of stitches and fractions of a stitch that make up 10 cm (4 in.) of knitting.

You must work a test strip before you begin. This can always be unravelled and used again.

Using the yarn you've chosen, and:

- 4 mm needles – for small 77–87 cm (30–34 in.) garments
- 5 mm needles – for medium-sized 87–102 cm (34–40 in.) garments

- 6 mm needles – for large 102–112 cm (40–44 in.) garments

cast on 25 sts.
Work 25 rows using the type of stitch or pattern you've chosen (e.g. stocking stitch, fancy rib, Fair Isle).

Change to:

- 5 mm needles (small)
- 6 mm needles (medium)
- 7 mm needles (large)

and do this again.

Work a further 25 rows using:

- 6 mm (small)
- 7 mm (medium)
- 7.5 mm (large)

and cast off.

Ideally, the tension square should be left for twelve hours before being measured because the yarn needs time to settle down to its natural tension.

Lay the test strip on a firm, flat surface and, being careful not to stretch it, mark out a 10 cm square with pins.

> ### HANDY TIP
> *Always make your test strip in the stitch you plan to use for the sweater. The dimensions of stocking stitch, ribs, lace stitches and Fair Isle patterns will all be quite different, even though you've used the same-sized needles.*

Count how many stitches and rows you've knitted for each size of needle, then check with the chart below to find the correct gauge for your size of sweater.

To fit chest		Gauge
77–82 cm	(30–32 in.)	16 sts : 20 rows
82–87 cm	(32–34 in.)	15 sts : 19 rows
87–92 cm	(34–36 in.)	14 sts : 18 rows
92–97 cm	(36–38 in.)	13 sts : 17 rows
97–102 cm	(38–40 in.)	12 sts : 16 rows
102–107 cm	(40–42 in.)	11 sts : 15 rows
107–112 cm	(42–44 in.)	10 sts : 14 rows

Because the gauge is partly determined by the tension you put on the yarn (a tight knitter will produce a smaller square than a loose knitter) you may find that none of the needles you've used in your test strip is quite right. Keep experimenting. The correct gauge may fall between two of these needle sizes. If your gauge is too small, try a larger needle; if it's too big, try a smaller needle.

NOTE: A knitting needle conversion chart, giving continental (mm), British and US sizes, appears on page 161.

> **HANDY TIP**
> *When selecting sweater size, find a sweater that you know fits well. Lay it out flat and measure the chest.*

Altering the length of a pattern

If you want to alter the length of the garment, make it shorter or turn it into a dress, add or subtract the required number of rows.

For example: you want to make a dress 92–97 cm (36–38 in.) chest and 77 cm (30 in.) from the hem to the armhole.

A 92–97 cm garment uses gauge 13 sts : 17 rows/10 cm, so, the number of rows from the hem to the armhole will be

$$\frac{77 \ (\text{cm}) \ \times \ 17 \ (\text{rows})}{10 \ (\text{cm})} = 130 \text{ rows}$$

Or, for a three-quarter-length sleeve, take off about 20 rows from the bottom of the sleeve pattern.

Collars, cuffs and welts can all be shortened or lengthened in the same way.

REMEMBER: *you must make a test strip* each time you use a new yarn. Each yarn behaves differently with a given size of needle, so make sure you're working at the correct gauge each time you make a new garment.

All ribs, collars, cuffs, welts and button bands are made on needles two sizes smaller than those used for the body of the garment. For example, a sweater which requires 5 mm needles will need 4 mm needles for the cuffs and welt.

HANDY TIP

When knitting a large number of stitches (e.g. for a dolman or one-piece design), use a circular needle. This allows the main weight of the garment to slip into the centre of the wire and it can then rest in your lap.

NOTE: A conversion chart for metric and imperial measurements appears on page 161. Where appropriate, both have been given in the text, but readers should keep to *either* metric *or* imperial measures and not attempt to change from one to the other, as equivalents are rounded off.

Table of length and weight in commercial mohair yarns

KEY:

A	–	acrylic	M	–	mohair	TS – tussah silk	
Ac	–	acrilan	MP	–	metallic polyester	V – viscose	
Alp	–	alpaca	N	–	nylon	W – wool	
C	–	cotton	P	–	polyamid		
KM	–	kid mohair	S	–	silk		

FINE YARNS	Country	Metres/10g	Composition
Royal Mohair (Katia)	Spain	37 m	58%KM 42%A
Geisha (Esslinger Wolle)	West Germany	35 m	85%P 15%M
Saratoga (Tahki)	USA	35 m	55%M 15%S 20%W 10%P
Phil'douce (Phildar)	France	34 m	75%A 20%KM 5%W
Mohair Multi (Filatura de Crosa)	Italy	32 m	60%M 40%A
Nuvoletta (Filatura de Crosa)	Italy	32 m	70%M 30%A
Mohair et Soie (Pingouin)	France	30 m	85%KM 15%S
Mohair 50 (Pingouin)	France	30 m	50%M 40%A 10%W
Mohair Kid 80 (Schaffhauser)	USA	29 m	80%KM 20%A
No. 1 Kid (Georges Picaud)	France	28 m	80%KM 20%A

FINE YARNS	Country	Metres/10g	Composition
Evening (3 Suisses)	Great Britain	25 m	60%A 35%W 5%M
Geisha (Katia)	Spain	25 m	75%A 25%M
Mille et une Nuits (Pingouin)	France & Great Britain	25 m	37%W 30%M 25%A 5%P 3%N
Mohair Seide (Woll & Seidenkontor)	Switzerland	25 m	70%KM 30%TS
Tahki 80/20 (Tahki)	USA	25 m	80%M 20%A

MEDIUM YARNS	Country	Metres/10g	Composition
Filigree Supreme (Emu)	Great Britain	22 m	77%M 14%W 9%N
Finesse (Argyll)	Great Britain	22 m	78%M 13%W 9%N
Gypsy (Jaeger)	Great Britain	22 m	71%M 13%W 9%N 7%A
Mongora (Margarita)	Spain	22 m	86%M 8%P 6%W
Woollybear Mohair (Patricia Roberts)	Great Britain	22 m	100%M
5 Star (Lister)	Great Britain	22 m	81%M 14%W 5%N
Amalfi (Wendy)	Great Britain	21 m	65%A 30%M 5%C
Kid Mohair (Patons)	Australia	21 m	40%M 40%W 20%KM
Renaissance (Bernat)	USA	21 m	40%M 29%A 14%W 17%MP
Tamara (3 Suisses)	Great Britain	21 m	40%M 30%W 30%A
Venetian (Bernat)	USA	21 m	71%A 16%M 13%N
Venetian Frost (Bernat)	USA	21 m	55%A 29%N 16%M
Crucci Mohair (Crucci)	New Zealand	20 m	67%M 28%W 5%N
Jonelle (John Lewis Partnership)	Great Britain	20 m	70%M 25%W 5%N

MEDIUM YARNS	Country	Metres/10g	Composition
Lugano (Hayfield Textiles)	Great Britain	20 m	51%M 37.5%N 11.5%A
Lugano Fancy (Hayfield Textiles)	Great Britain	20 m	52%M 40%A 4%N 4%P
Miri (BBB)	Italy	20 m	59%M 40%A 4%N 4%P
Mohair 3 Suisses (3 Suisses)	Great Britain	20 m	67%M 28%W 5%P
Molly (BBB)	Italy	20 m	70%M 30%W
Myth (Cleckheaton)	Australia	20 m	93%KM 7%N
Opaline (Laines Jacques Fonty)	France	20 m	40%M 57%W 3%P
Babytall (Filatura di Crosa)	Italy	19 m	80%KM 20%A
Butterfly (Emu)	Great Britain	19 m	62%M 24%A 14%N
Kashmir Mohair (Thorobred Sheepjeswol)	Australia	19 m	80%W 20%M
Nocturne (Sirdar)	Great Britain	19 m	77%M 13%W 10%N
Serona Mohair (Thorobred Sheepjeswol)	Australia	19 m	67%M 28%W 5%N
Banquise (Pingouin)	France & Great Britain	18 m	70%M 20%N 10%W
Fiamma (Filatura di Crosa)	Italy	18 m	26%M 44%C 16%A 11%W 3%N
Gabi (Schoeller Wolle)	West Germany	18 m	60%M 30%A 10%W
Gold (Jaeger)	Great Britain	18 m	84%M 16%N
Intrigue (Pingouin)	France & Great Britain	18 m	42%P 25%W 18%A 15%M
Laureate (Phildar)	France	18 m	60%C 20%KM 15%A 5%W
Luxury Mohair (Patons)	Australia	18 m	74%M/W 26%N
Mohair 2000 (Filatura di Crosa)	Italy	18 m	91%M 7%W 2%N
Mohair Tweed (Infitex)	Spain	18 m	65%M 33%A 2%P

MEDIUM YARNS	Country	Metres/10g	Composition
Riverline (British Mohair Spinners)	Great Britain	18 m	78%M 13%W 9%N
Siberia (Patons)	Great Britain	18 m	77.5%A 12%C 8.5%M 2%N
Azor (BBB)	Italy	17 m	65%W 29%M 6%V
Medium 1 (Lesotho Handspun)	Lesotho	17 m	100%M
Melody (Villawool)	Australia	16 m	69%A 13%M 13%W 5%N
Pebblespun (Bernat)	USA	16 m	70%W 22%M 8%N
Contrastes (Pingouin)	France	15 m	64%V 25%M 11%W
Mohair Amour (Patons)	Australia	15 m	73%M/W 27%N
Solo with Mohair (Patons)	Great Britain	15 m	56%A 24%W 20%M
Harmonie (Filatura di Crosa)	Italy	14 m	85%M 13%W 2%N
Charm (Patons)	Australia	14 m	36%W 32%M 32%A
Harmonie Lana (Filatura di Crosa)	Italy	14 m	78%M 12%W 5%V 3%P 2%N
Musetta (Bernat)	USA	14 m	48%W 36%M 16%A
Thistledown (Brunswick Yarns)	Canada	14 m	42%Alp 42%M 16%N

THICK YARNS	Country	Metres/10g	Composition
Fifi (Georges Picaud)	France	12 m	51%C 40%M 9%A
Mohair Buffo (Filatura di Crosa)	Italy	12 m	72%M 28%W
Princess (Patons)	USA	12 m	59%A 17.5%M 12.5%N 11%W
Coriandolo (Filatura di Crosa)	Italy	11 m	46%M 42%Ac 10%A 2%P

THICK YARNS	Country	Metres/10g	Composition
Flash Dance (3 Suisses)	Great Britain	10 m	60%A 25%W 5%M
Royal Mohair (Infitex)	Spain	10 m	90%KM 10%P
Ribbon Mist (Jaeger)	Great Britain	9 m	61%V 22%A 16%M 1%N
Ribbon Mohair (Patons)	Australia	9 m	47%V 24%W 18%M 10%A 1%N
Rosita (Filatura di Crosa)	Italy	9 m	54%M 36%A 10%W
Enchante (Patons)	Australia	8 m	47%M 30%A 16%P 7%W
La de Dion Bouton (Welcomme)	France	7 m	64%A 32%M 2%W 2%P
le Mohair (Lesotho Handspun)	Lesotho	7 m	100%M

2

BASIC PATTERNS

ROUND NECK

Back

Using the smaller needles cast on 65 sts.
Rib 11 rows.
Next row: Inc 10 sts evenly across this row purlwise (75 sts).
Change to the larger needles and pattern 50 rows.
Decrease for armholes as follows:
Cast off 4 sts at beg of next 2 rows.
Cast off 2 sts at beg of next 2 rows.
Cast off 1 st at beg of next 2 rows.
††
Continue to follow pattern for 32 rows.
Shape shoulders as follows:
Pattern to last 6 sts, turn.
Repeat.
Pattern to last 12 sts, turn.
Repeat.
Pattern to last 18 sts, turn.
Repeat.
Cast off centre 25 sts.
Leave the 18 sts of each shoulder on a spare needle ready for grafting.

Front

As for back until ††.
Continue in pattern for 23 rows.
Shape neck and shoulders as follows:
Pattern 24 sts, cast off 13 sts, pattern to end.
Continue on right side of garment.
*Pattern 1 row.
Cast off 3 sts at beg of next row.
Pattern 1 row.

Cast off 2 sts at beg of next row.
Pattern 1 row.
Cast off 1 st at beg of next row.
Pattern 3 rows.
Pattern to last 6 sts, turn.
Pattern 1 row.
Pattern to last 12 sts, turn.
Pattern 1 row.
Leave these 18 sts on a spare needle.**

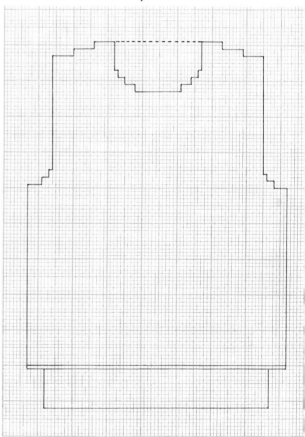

With right side of garment facing you, repeat the neck and shoulder instructions from * to ** on the left side, beginning at the armhole edge.

Making up
Sew in all loose ends.
Graft together shoulder seams.
Set chosen sleeve into armhole.
Sew side seams.
Attach collar according to type of collar chosen.

V-NECK

Back
Using the smaller needles cast on 64 sts.
Rib 11 rows.
Next row: Inc 10 sts evenly across this row purlwise (74 sts).
Change to larger needles and pattern 50 rows.
Decrease for armholes as follows:
Cast off 4 sts at beg of next 2 rows.
Cast off 2 sts at beg of next 2 rows.
Cast off 1 st at beg of next 2 rows.
††
Continue to follow pattern for 32 rows.
Shape shoulders as follows:
Pattern to last 6 sts, turn.
Repeat.
Pattern to last 12 sts, turn.
Repeat.
Pattern to last 18 sts, turn.
Repeat.
Cast off centre 24 sts.
Leave the 18 sts of each shoulder on a spare needle ready for grafting.

Front
As for back until ††.
Continue in pattern for 13 rows.
Shape neck and shoulders as follows:
Pattern 29 sts, cast off 2 sts, pattern to end.
Continue on right side of garment.
*Pattern 1 row.
Cast off 1 st at beg of next and every alternate row until 20 sts remain (finishing at neck edge).

Next row: Cast off 1 st, pattern 12 sts, turn.
Pattern 1 row.
Cast off 1 st, pattern 5 sts, turn.
Pattern 1 row.
Leave these 18 sts on a spare needle.**
With right side of garment facing you, repeat the neck and shoulder instructions from * to ** on the left side, beginning at the armhole edge.

Making up
Sew in all loose ends.
Graft together shoulder seam.
Set chosen sleeve into armhole.
Sew side seams.
Attach collar according to type of collar chosen.

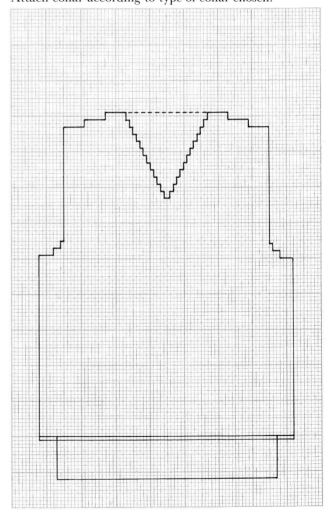

CROSSOVER JACKET

Back

Using the smaller needles cast on 70 sts.
Rib 11 rows.
Next row: Inc 10 sts evenly across this row purlwise (80 sts).
Change to the larger needles and pattern 64 rows.
Decrease for armholes as follows:
Cast off 4 sts at beg of next 2 rows.
Cast off 2 sts at beg of next 2 rows.

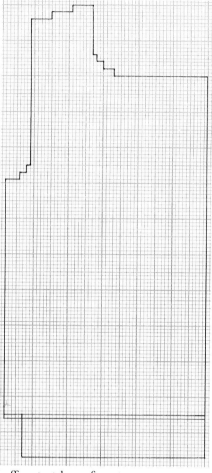

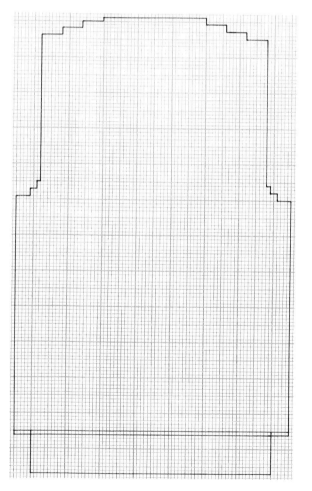

Cast off 1 st at beg of next 2 rows.
Continue to follow pattern for 40 rows.
Shape shoulders as follows:
Pattern to last 6 sts, turn.
Repeat.
Pattern to last 12 sts, turn.
Repeat.
Pattern to last 18 sts, turn.
Repeat.
Cast off centre 30 sts.
Leave the 18 sts of each shoulder on a spare needle ready for grafting.

Right front

Using the smaller needles cast on 53 sts.
Rib 11 rows.
Next row: Inc 5 sts evenly across this row (58 sts).
†Change to the larger needles and pattern 65 rows.

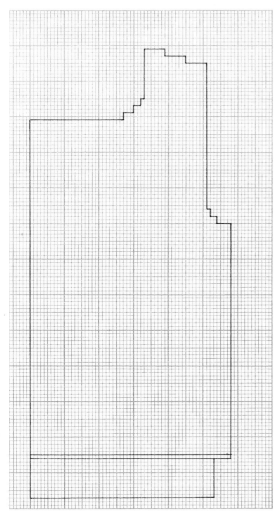

Decrease for armholes as follows:
Cast off 4 sts at beg of next row.
Pattern 1 row.
Cast off 2 sts at beg of next row.
Pattern 1 row.
Cast off 1 st at beg of next row.
Continue to follow pattern for 24 rows.
Shape neck as follows:
Cast off 27 sts at beg of next row.
Pattern 1 row.
Cast off 3 sts at beg of next row.
Pattern 1 row.
Cast off 2 sts at beg of next row.
Pattern 1 row.
Cast off 1 st at beg of next row.
Pattern 9 rows.

Shape shoulders as follows:
Pattern to last 6 sts, turn.
Pattern 1 row.
Pattern to last 12 sts, turn.
Pattern 1 row.
Pattern to last 6 sts, turn.
Pattern 1 row.
Leave these 18 sts on a spare needle ready for grafting.

Left front

Work as for right front to †.
After 64 rows dec for armholes.
Continue as for right front.

Making up

Sew in all loose ends.
Graft together shoulder seams.
Sew side seams.
Set chosen sleeve into armhole.
Sew button bands in place (stretching them slightly to fit).
Sew buttons in place.
Attach chosen collar.

ONE-PIECE JACKET

Body

Using the smaller needles cast on 140 sts.
Rib 14 rows.
Next row: Inc 20 sts evenly across this row purlwise (160 sts).
†Change to the larger needles and pattern 65 rows.
Divide for armholes as follows:
Pattern 35 sts, cast off 10 sts, pattern 70 sts, cast off 10 sts, pattern to end.

Right front

Continue on first 35 sts only.
*1st row: Pattern to end.
2nd row: Cast off 3 sts at armhole edge.
3rd row: Pattern to end.
4th row: Cast off 2 sts at armhole edge.

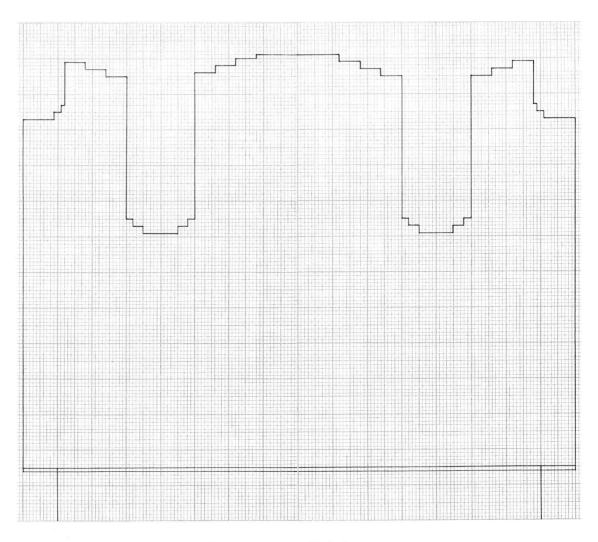

Continue on these 30 sts for 26 rows (finishing at neck edge).

Shape neck as follows:
Cast off 9 sts at neck edge, pattern to end.
Pattern 1 row.
Cast off 2 sts at neck edge, pattern to end.
Pattern 1 row.
Cast off 1 st at neck edge, pattern to end.
Pattern 8 rows (finishing at neck edge).

Shape shoulders as follows:
Pattern to last 6 sts, turn.
Pattern 1 row.
Pattern to last 12 sts, turn.
Pattern 1 row.
Leave these 18 sts on a spare needle.**

Left front
With right side of garment facing, join mohair to the outside edge and repeat instructions from * to **.

Centre back
With right side of garment facing, join mohair to the centre 70 sts.
Cast off 3 sts at beg of next 2 rows.
Cast off 2 sts at beg of next 2 rows (60 sts).
Continue for 38 rows.

Shape shoulders as follows:
Pattern to last 6 sts, turn.
Pattern to last 6 sts, turn.
Pattern to last 12 sts, turn.

Pattern to last 12 sts, turn.
Pattern 6 sts, cast off 24 sts.
Leave the sts from both shoulders on a spare needle ready for grafting.††

Making up

Sew in all loose ends.
Graft shoulder seams together.
Set chosen sleeve into armhole.
Attach button bands and buttons.
Attach collar according to type of collar chosen.

REVERSIBLE ONE-PIECE JACKET

(This is made by first making the one-piece jacket and then knitting a lining using the same welt as the main body. The two pieces of knitting should be worked so that the wrong sides face each other.)

Using the larger needles, with the wrong side of the knitting facing you, cast on edge uppermost and, beginning at the right-hand side of the work, pick up the 160 sts from the increase row above the welt.
Follow the body pattern from † to ††.
Work the sleeves by picking up the sts on the increase row above the cuff and then following the sleeve pattern in the same way.

Making up

Sew in all loose ends.
Graft shoulder seams of main body together.
Graft shoulder seams of lining together.
Arrange body and lining in place and then oversew around the neck edge, up the fronts, and around the armholes, making sure the body and lining are not stretched.
Attach the *sleeves* by first sewing up the side seams of the main sleeves and then the side seams of the lining on the inside.
Then overlay (by about 2 cm/¾ in.) and pin the top curve of the main sleeves on the outside of the main body armholes and sew in place.
Turn the jacket inside out, overlay and pin the lining sleeve on the outside of the lining armhole, and sew in place.
A backstitch close to the edge of the curve gives a firmer seam than oversewing.
Attach *armbands* in the usual way.
Collars (except 'ruff', 'horizontal cable', 'roll and bow' and 'ridged shawl collar') can be made with a Y-shaped band to slot the neck edge into:

After making the collar:

With the wrong side of the collar facing you, cast on edge uppermost, and beginning at the right side, pick up the sts along the 4th row from the cast on edge.
St st 3 rows, beginning with a purl row.
Cast off.
Sandwich this 'Y' around the neck edge and sew in place on both the outside and the inside of the garment.
The 'roll and bow' and 'scarf' collars are made and attached in the usual way.

BLOUSE SLEEVE
(suitable for 'round neck' or 'V-neck' bodies)

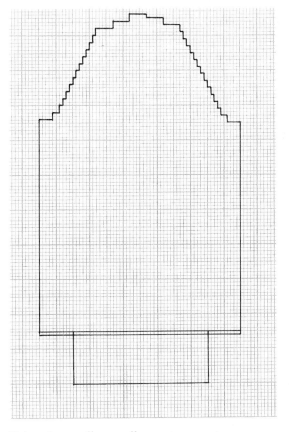

Using the smaller needles cast on 40 sts.
Rib 14 rows.
Next row: Inc 20 sts evenly across this row (60 sts).
Change to the larger needles.
Pattern 60 rows.

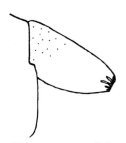

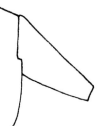

Shape top as follows:
Cast off 4 sts at beg of next 2 rows.
Cast off 2 sts at beg of next 2 rows.
K2 tog at beg of next 23 rows.
Cast off 5 sts at beg of next 5 rows.

SHAPED SLEEVE
(suitable for 'round neck' or 'V-neck' bodies)

Change to the larger needles.
Increase 1 st at each end of every 8th row 6 times
(62 sts).
Pattern 11 rows.
Shape top as follows:
Cast off 4 sts at beg of next 2 rows.
Cast off 2 sts at beg of next 2 rows.
K2 tog at beg of next 25 rows.
Cast off 5 sts at beg of next 5 rows.

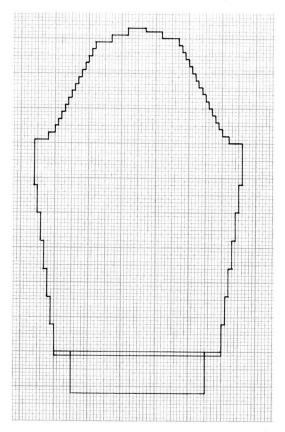

Using the smaller needles cast on 40 sts.
Rib 11 rows.
Next row: Inc 10 sts evenly across this row (50 sts).

SHIRT SLEEVES *(suitable for 'round neck',
'V-neck', 'crossover' and 'one-piece' bodies)*

Right sleeve
Using the smaller needles cast on 42 sts.
Rib 5 rows.
***Buttonhole row:**
Rib 4 sts, yrn, p2 tog, rib to end.
Rib 7 rows.
Next row: Inc 16 sts evenly across this row (58 sts).
Change to the larger needles.
Inc 1 st at each end of every 10th row 5 times (68 sts).
**Pattern 9 rows.
Dec for top shaping as follows:
Pattern 17 sts, cast off 7 sts, pattern to end.
Continue on left side of sleeve only.
Pattern 1 row.
Dec 1 st at beg of next and following alt rows 17 times (28 sts).
Dec 1 st at each end of next 5 rows (18 sts).

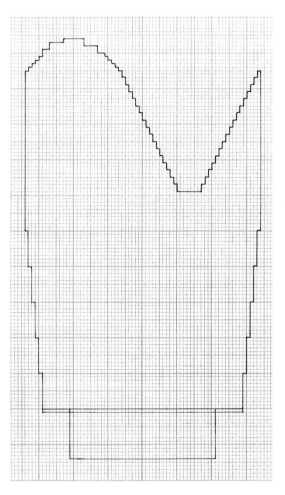

Making up

Sew outer sleeve seams to within 10 cm (4 in.) of the cuff edge.
(Chain stitch on the outside of the seam to highlight the detail.)
Set sleeve into armhole.
Sew button on to cuff.

HUGE SLEEVE (*suitable for 'round neck', 'V-neck', 'crossover' and 'one-piece' bodies*)

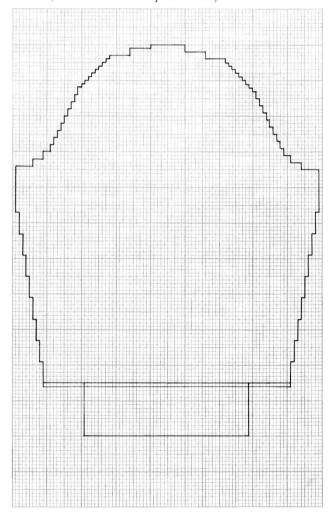

Cast off 2 sts at beg of next 2 rows.
Cast off 4 sts at beg of next 2 rows.
Cast off remaining 6 sts.
Join mohair to right side of sleeve at outside edge.
Pattern 1 row.
Decrease 1 st at beg of next and every alt row until no sts remain.

Left sleeve

As for right sleeve to *.
Buttonhole row:
Rib 36 sts, yrn, k2 tog, rib to end.
Continue as for right sleeve to **.
Pattern 10 rows.
Continue as for right sleeve but reversing 'right' and 'left'.

Using the smaller needles cast on 48 sts.
Rib 14 rows.
Next row: Inc 24 sts evenly across this row (72 sts).
Change to the larger needles.

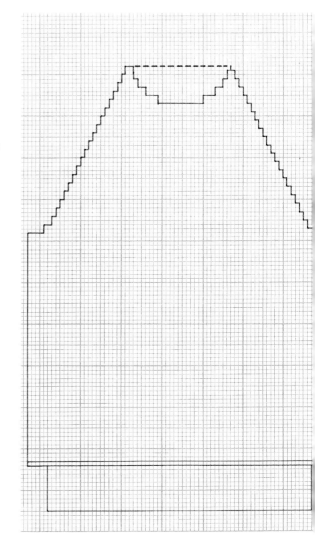

Increase 1 st at each end of every 6th row 8 times (88 sts).
Pattern 11 rows.
Shape top as follows:
Cast off 5 sts at beg of next 2 rows.
Cast off 3 sts at beg of next 2 rows.
Cast off 2 sts at beg of next 2 rows.
K2 tog at beg of next 18 rows.
K2 tog at both ends of next 8 rows.
Cast off 6 sts at beg of next 4 rows.
Cast off 10 sts.

RAGLAN BODY

Back
Using the smaller needles cast on 65 sts.
Rib 11 rows.
Next row: Inc 10 sts evenly across this row (75 sts).
Change to the larger needles and pattern 54 rows.
Decrease for armholes as follows:
Cast off 4 sts at beg of next 2 rows.
Cast off 2 sts at beg of next 2 rows.
†† Dec 1 st at beg of next 36 rows (27 sts).
Cast off.

Front
As for back until ††.
Dec 1 st at beg of next 28 rows.
Next row: Dec 1 st, pattern 11 sts, cast off 11 sts, pattern to end.
Continue on right side of neck as follows:
*1st row: Dec 1 st, pattern to end.
2nd row: Cast off 3 sts, pattern to end.
3rd row: Dec 1 st, pattern to end.
4th row: Cast off 2 sts, pattern to end.
5th row: Dec 1 st, pattern to end.

6th row: Cast off 1 st, pattern to end.
7th row: Dec 1 st, pattern to end.
Cast off **
With right side of garment facing you, repeat the neck and shoulder instructions from * to ** on the left side.

Making up
Sew in all loose ends.
Set sleeves into armholes.
Sew side seams.
Attach collar according to type of collar chosen.

RAGLAN SLEEVE
(suitable for raglan body only)

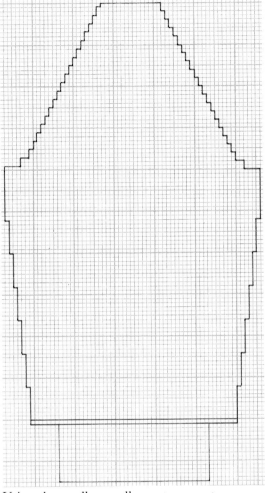

Using the smaller needles cast on 37 sts.
Rib 14 rows.
Next row: Inc 14 sts evenly across this row (51 sts).
Change to the larger needles.
Increase 1 st at each end of every 8th row 6 times (63 sts).
Pattern 11 rows.
Shape top as follows:
Cast off 4 sts at beg of next 2 rows.
Cast off 2 sts at beg of next 2 rows.
K2 tog at beg of next 36 rows.
Cast off.

DOLMAN

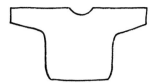

Body
Using the smaller needles cast on 66 sts.
Rib 14 rows.
Next row: Inc 10 sts evenly across this row (76 sts).
Change to the larger needles and pattern 50 rows.
Inc for sleeves as follows:
Cast on 6 sts at beg of next 2 rows.
Cast on 8 sts at beg of next 4 rows.
Cast on 10 sts at beg of next 6 rows (180 sts).
After 10 rows divide for neck as follows:
Pattern 80 sts, cast off 20 sts, pattern to end.
Continue on right side of garment.
*1st row: Pattern to end.
2nd row: Cast off 3 sts at neck edge, pattern to end.
3rd row: Pattern to end.
4th row: Cast off 2 sts at neck edge, pattern to end.
5th row: Pattern to end.
6th row: Cast off 1 st at neck edge, pattern to end.
After 7 rows inc for front of neck as follows:
1st row: Cast on 1 st at neck edge, pattern to end.
2nd row: Pattern to end.
3rd row: Cast on 2 sts at neck edge, pattern to end.
4th row: Pattern to end.
5th row: Cast on 3 sts at neck edge, pattern to end **
6th row: Pattern to end (finishing at neck edge).
Put these sts on to a spare needle and repeat the instructions from * to ** on the left side of the garment, beginning at the cuff edge.
(Check that both sides of the garment have completed the same amount of pattern.)
Next row: Pattern the 80 sts of the right side, cast on 20 sts, join mohair to the sts from the left side and pattern these 80 sts (180 sts).
Pattern 18 rows.
Dec for sleeve as follows:
Cast off 10 sts at beg of next 6 rows.
Cast off 8 sts at beg of next 4 rows.
Cast off 6 sts at beg of next 2 rows (76 sts).
Pattern 50 rows.

33

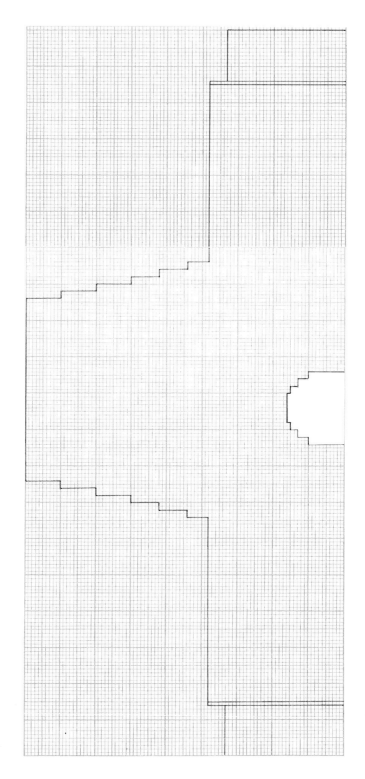

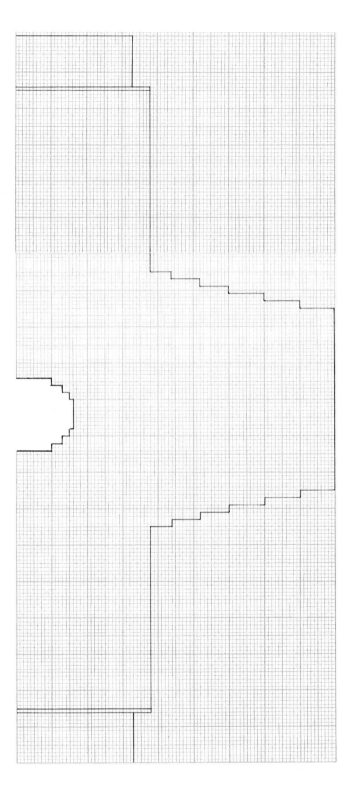

Next row: Dec 10 sts evenly across this row (66 sts).

Change to the smaller needles and rib 14 rows.

Cast off using a size larger needle.

Cuffs (2)

Using the smaller needles cast on 36 sts.

Rib 14 rows – do not cast off.

Graft the cuffs to the sleeve.

Making up

Sew in all loose ends.

Sew on the selected collar in the appropriate manner.

Sew the side seams and sleeve seams.

NOTE: If you do experiment further and decide to use the dolman pattern for a very small child, it may be necessary to omit the cuffs and turn the sleeves under instead.

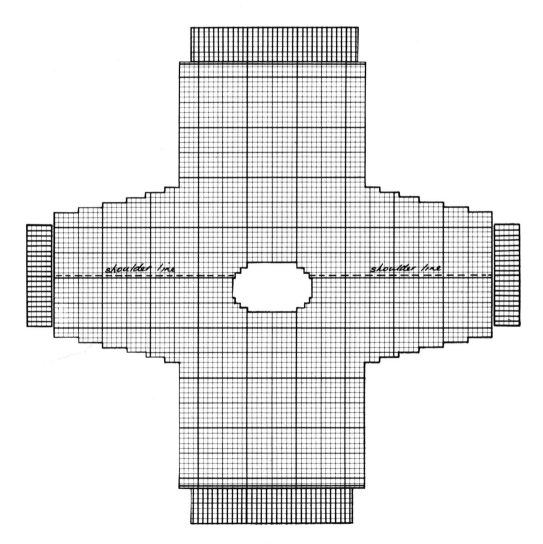

LAYOUT OF DOLMAN PATTERN

(1 square = 2 sts and 2 rows)

Dolman sweater (page 36)

- Body and sleeves of dolman sweater are worked in one piece.
- Begin knitting at the bottom of the front welt. Cast off at the bottom of the neck welt.
- Graft the cuffs on to the sleeves.
- Attach the chosen collar.

Dolman cardigan

- Draw a line down the centre front of the dolman pattern to separate the fronts.
- Work the right front as far as the neck line and leave it on a spare needle. Repeat with the left front.
- Work across the right front, cast on 20 sts, then work across the left front (180 sts).
- Continue to work down the back, following the sleeve decrease shapings and the welt decreases.
- Graft the cuffs on to the sleeves.
- Attach the button bands.
- Attach the chosen collar.

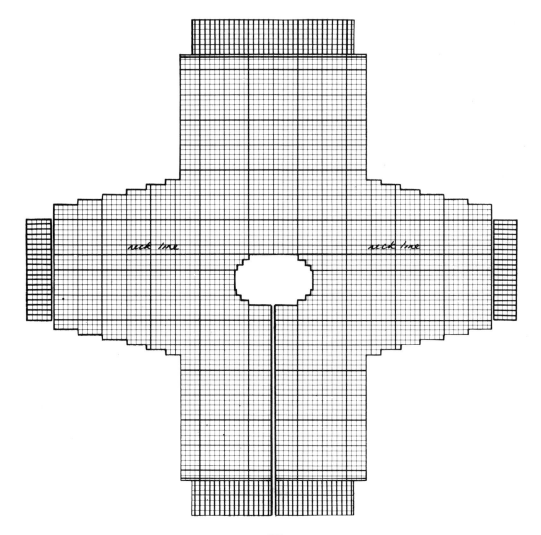

· 3 ·

COLLARS, CUFFS,
WELTS and EXTRAS

COLLARS

Use needles two sizes smaller than those used for the body and sleeves.

When making a collar, the same number of sts is used for all the *sweaters*. The number of sts for cardigans (C) or for the Crossover jacket (CJ) is indicated separately.

ELIZABETHAN COLLAR

For all garments.
Cast on 13 sts and k 2 rows.

If the Elizabethan collar is for a cardigan or jacket, make a buttonhole (k2, yrn, k2 tog) on 9th row at beginning of collar for a man's garment, on 9th row at the end of the collar for a woman's garment.

1st row: K13.
2nd row: P10, turn.
3rd row: K10.
4th row: As 2nd row.
5th row: As 3rd row.
6th row: As 2nd row.
7th row: As 3rd row.
8th row: P13.
9th row: K13.
10th row: K10, turn.

11th row: P10.
12th row: As 10th row.
13th row: As 11th row.
14th row: As 10th row.
15th row: As 11th row.
16th row: P13.
Repeat these 16 rows until the collar is long enough to go round the neckline.
K 2 rows.
Cast off loosely.

If the Elizabethan collar is to be used on a sweater, sew together the short edges and position this seam at the centre back of the neck edge.

For jackets or cardigans, position the short edges in line with the front edges of the garment after the button band has been attached.

Place the narrower, st st edge of the collar around the outside of the neck edge, allowing it to overlap slightly, and sew in place. Catch down the raw inside edge of the neck.

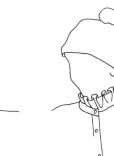  

FLUTED COLLAR

the 4th st, or 4th st from the end if for a man's garment, if fluted collar is for a cardigan or jacket.
Next row: P.
Next row: K.
Next row: P.
Cast off loosely knitwise.

If the fluted collar is to be used on a sweater, sew together the short edges and position this seam at the centre back of the neck edge.

For jackets or cardigans, position the short edges in line with the front edges of the garment after the button band has been attached.

Place the cast off edge of the collar around the outside of the neck edge, allowing it to overlap slightly, and sew in place. Catch down the raw inside edge of the neck.

FRONT, SIDE AND BACK SLIT
(not suitable for jackets and cardigans)

Don't be put off by the number of cast on sts –
many of these disappear on the first row.
Cast on 254 (C282, CJ338) sts.
1st row: K1, *k2, p3 tog, k2*, k1 (182, C202, CJ242 sts).
Beginning with a P row, st st 9 rows.
Next row: Sl 1 on to a double-ended needle and lay at back of work, *sl 3 on to a second double-ended needle and lay at front of work, sl 3 on to first double-ended needle and lay at back of work*, sl last st on to the back needle.
Next row: Return to beg of row and lay the two double-ended needles alongside one another, k1, graft all the sts tog knitwise to the last st, k1 (92, C102, CJ122 sts).
Next row (wrong side if a short stand-up collar, right side if a polo-length collar): K.
Next row: K – make a buttonhole (yrn, k2 tog) on

Choose a rib from the section on stitch patterns.
Cast on 90 sts.
Rib until collar is a suitable length.
Next row (wrong side if a short stand-up collar, right side if a polo-length collar): K.
Next row: K.
Next row: P.

Next row: K.
Next row: P.
Cast off loosely knitwise.

Place the cast off edge of the collar around the outside of the neck edge, allowing the st st band to overlap the neck edge (leaving the short edges of the collar at the front, side or back as you prefer), and sew in place. Catch down the raw inside edge of the neck.

OVERLAY SLIT
(not suitable for jackets and cardigans)

Choose a rib from the section on stitch patterns.
Cast on 106 sts.
Rib until collar is a suitable length.
Next row (wrong side if a short stand-up collar, right side if a polo-length collar): K.
Next row: K.
Next row: P.
Next row: K.
Next row: P.
Cast off loosely knitwise.

Place the cast off edge of the collar around the outside of the neck edge, allowing the st st band to overlap the neck edge and overlapping the short edges of the collar a little off centre at the front. Sew in place. Catch down the raw inside edge of the neck.

POLO WITH OR WITHOUT TASSLES

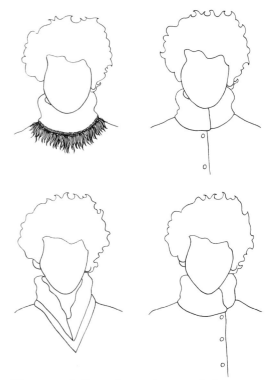

Choose a rib from the section on stitch patterns.
Cast on 90 (C100, CJ120) sts.
Rib until collar is a suitable length.
Next row (wrong side if a short stand-up collar, right side if a polo-length collar): K.
Next row: K – make a buttonhole (yrn, k2 tog) on the 4th st, or 4th st from the end if for a man's garment, if polo collar is for a cardigan or jacket.
Next row: P.
Next row: K.
Next row: P.
Cast off loosely knitwise.

If the polo collar is to be used on a sweater, sew together the short edges and position this seam at the centre back of the neck edge.

For jackets or cardigans, position the short edges in line with the front edges of the garment after the button band has been attached.

Place the cast off edge of the collar around the outside of the neck edge, allowing the st st band to overlap the neck edge. Sew in place. Catch down the raw inside edge of the neck. Attach tassels to the lower edge of the polo collar.

BUTTONED COLLAR

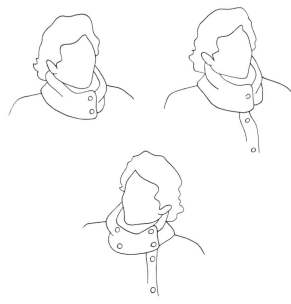

Choose a rib from the section on stitch patterns.
Cast on 90 (C100, CJ120) sts.
1st to 8th rows: Rib.
9th row: Rib 3, yrn, k2 tog, rib to end.
10th row: Rib.
These 10 rows form the pattern for the collar.
Continue to the required length.
Next row (with buttonholes lying at right-hand side of work for a man's garment, left-hand side for a woman's garment): K.
Next row: K – make a buttonhole (yrn, k2 tog) in line with the previously made buttonholes.
Next row: P.
Next row: K.
Next row: P.
Cast off loosely knitwise.
Place the cast off edge of the collar around the outside of the neck edge, allowing the st st band to overlap the neck edge.

If the buttoned collar is to be used on a sweater, position the short edges of the collar at the centre front or shoulder seam of the neck edge, overlapping the buttonhole edge on the inside of the neck.

Once the collar is rolled over the buttons will appear on the outside.

For jackets or cardigans, position the short edges in line with the front edges of the garment after the button band has been attached.

Sew in place. Catch down the raw inside edge. Sew buttons in place.

DETACHABLE YOKE
(not suitable for 'crossover jacket')

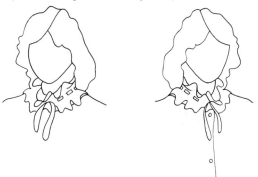

Cast on 114 (C138) sts.
1st row: P1, k1, *p2, k1*, p1.
2nd row: K1, p1, *k2, p1*, k1.
These two rows form the rib pattern.
Continue in rib for 15 rows ending in a first pattern row.
Eyelet hole row: K1, p1, *yrn, sl 1, k1, psso, p1* k1.
Work 6 more rows in rib pattern.
Cast off loosely in rib pattern.
Make a chain (about 95 cm/37 in. long for an adult's garment, shorter for a child's) and thread it through the eyelet holes to tie at centre front.
Make 2 pom-poms and sew to ends of chain.

VERTICAL CABLE

Cast on 90 (C100, CJ120) sts.
1st row: *K1, p1, k6, p1, k1*
2nd row: *P1, k1, p6, k1, p1*
3rd row: As 1st row.
4th row: As 2nd row.
5th row: *K1, p1, cable 6 fwd, p1, k1*.
6th row: As 2nd row.
7th row: As 1st row.

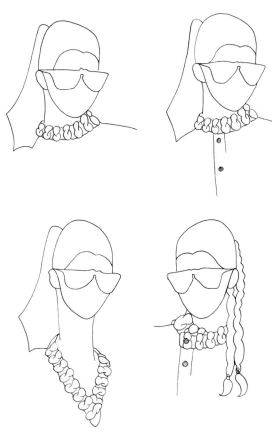

Place the cast off edge of the collar around the outside of the neck edge, allowing the st st band to overlap the neck edge. Sew in place. Catch down the raw inside edge of the neck.

HORIZONTAL CABLE

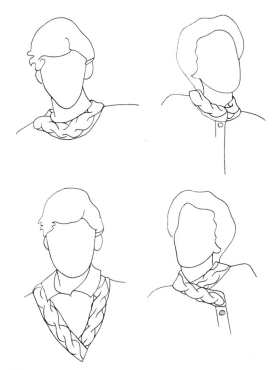

8th row: As 2nd row.

Repeat these 8 rows until the collar is the required length.

Next row (wrong side if a short stand-up collar, right side if a polo-length collar): K.

Next row: K – make a buttonhole (yrn, k2 tog) on the 4th st, or 4th st from the end if for a man's garment, if vertical cabled collar is for a cardigan or jacket.

Next row: P.

Next row: K.

Next row: P.

Cast off loosely knitwise.

If the vertical cabled collar is to be used on a sweater, sew together the short edges and position this seam at the centre back of the neck edge.

For jackets or cardigans, position the short edges in line with the front edges of the garment after the button band has been attached.

Cast on 10 sts.

1st row: P2, k6, p2.

2nd row: K2, p6, k2.

3rd row: As 1st row.

4th row: As 2nd row.

5th row: P2, cable 6 fwd, p2.

6th row: As 2nd row.

7th row: As 1st row.

8th row: As 2nd row.

Repeat these 8 rows (making a buttonhole – P2, k2, yrn, k2 tog, k2, p2 – on 3rd row if horizontal cable collar is for a cardigan or jacket) until the collar is long enough to go round the neckline. Cast off loosely.

If the horizontal cable collar is to be used on a sweater, sew together the short edges and position this seam at the centre back of the neck edge.

For jackets or cardigans, position the short edges in line with the front edges of the garment after the button band has been attached.

Place one edge of the collar around the outside of the neck edge, allowing it to overlap slightly and sew in place. Catch down the raw inside edge of the neck.

PICOT EDGE *(for sweaters)*

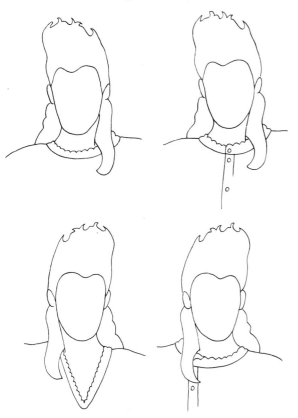

Cast on 92 sts.
St st 6 rows.
Next row: K1, *yrn, k2 tog*, k1.
Next row: Purl all the stitches.
St st 5 rows.
Cast off loosely.
Sew together the short edges and position this seam at the centre back of the neck edge.
Lay the collar around the outside of the neck edge, allowing it to overlap slightly, and sew in place. Fold in half and catch down the raw inside edge of the neck.

For cardigans:
Cast on C100 (CJ120) sts.
St st 2 rows.
3rd row: K2, yrn, k2 tog, k to end (this forms a buttonhole).
4th row: P.
5th row: K.
6th row: P.
7th row: K1, *yrn, k2 tog*, k1.
8th row: Purl all the stitches.
9th row: K.
10th row: P.
11th row: As 3rd row.
12th row: P.
13th row: K.
Cast off loosely.
Position the short edges of the collar in line with the front edges of the garment after the button band has been attached.
Lay the collar around the outside of the neck edge, allowing it to overlap slightly and sew in place. Fold in half. Catch down the raw inside edge of the neck and reinforce the buttonhole.

ROLL AND BOW *(for sweaters and cardigans)*

Cast on 8 sts.
St st until band is long enough to go round the neck, plus about 100 cm (39 in.) for an adult's garment, or 80 cm (31 in.) for a child's, for the tie.
Cast off.
Find the centre point of the band and place this in line with the centre back of the garment. Lay the band around the outside of the neck edge, allowing it to overlap slightly, and sew as far as the

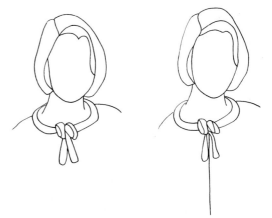

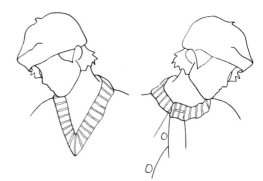

centre front on each side. Fold in half and catch down the raw inside edge of the neck. Tie the bow.

For crossover jacket:
Cast on 8 sts.
St st until band is long enough to go round the neck, plus 50 cm (20 in.) for an adult's garment, or 40 cm (16 in.) for a child's, for the tie.
Cast off loosely.
Beginning at the underlying jacket edge, lay the band around the outside of the neck edge, allowing it to overlap slightly and sew in place, leaving 50 cm (20 in.) for the tie. Fold in half and catch down the raw inside edge of the neck. Make another tie 50/40 cm (20/16 in.) long and attach this to the collar band in line with the crossover edge.

SWOLLEN RIB *or* GARTER STITCH COLLAR

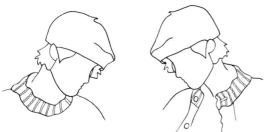

Cast on 90 (C100, CJ120) sts.
K1, p1 (rib) or k (garter st) for 20 rows (for cardigans and jackets make a buttonhole – yrn, k2 tog – on the 4th st of the 3rd and 9th rows).
Cast off loosely.

If the swollen rib is to be used on a sweater, sew together the short edges and position this seam at the centre back of the neck edge.

For jackets or cardigans, position the short edges in line with the front edges of the garment after the button band has been attached.

Place the cast off edge of the collar around the outside of the neck edge, allowing it to overlap slightly, and sew in place.

Fold the band in half and catch down the cast on edge at the inside of the neck edge.

Catch down the raw inside edge of the neck and reinforce the buttonhole if necessary.

COWL COLLARED HOOD
(for sweaters and crossover jacket)

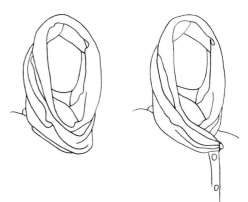

Cast on 90 (CJ120) sts.
St st 60 rows (or until collar is long enough to make a comfortable hood).
Next row (wrong side): K.
Next row: K – make a buttonhole (yrn, k2 tog) on the 4th st, or 4th st from the end if for a man's garment, if cowl collared hood is for a crossover jacket.
Next row: P.
Next row: K.

Next row: P.
Cast off loosely knitwise.

If the cowl collared hood is to be used on a sweater, sew together the short edges and position this seam at the centre back of the neck edge.

For the crossover jacket, position the short edges in line with the front edges of the garment after the button band has been attached. Using a double strand of yarn, about 60 cm (24 in.) long, pass a running stitch along the short edge of the collar and pull it as tightly as possible. Make a buttonhole loop on this edge. Repeat on the other short edge.

Place the cast off edge of the collar around the outside of the neck edge, allowing it to overlap slightly, and sew in place. Catch down the raw inside edge of the neck. The collar can be rolled down to form a cowl collar or up to make a hood.

SIMPLE RIBBED BAND

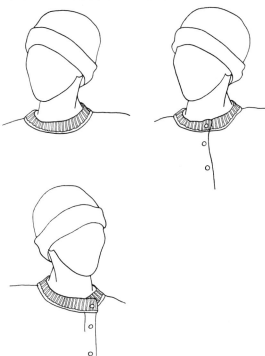

Cast on 90 (C100, CJ120) sts.
Rib (k1 p1) 8 rows.
Next row (wrong side): K.

Next row: K – make a buttonhole (yrn, k2 tog) on the 4th st, or 4th st from the end if for a man's garment, if ribbed band is for a cardigan or jacket.
Next row: P.
Next row: K.
Next row: P.
Cast off loosely knitwise.

If the simple ribbed band is to be used on a sweater, sew together the short edges and position this seam at the centre back of the neck edge.

For jackets or cardigans, position the short edges in line with the front edges of the garment after the button band has been attached.

Place the cast off edge of the collar around the outside of the neck edge, allowing it to overlap slightly, and sew in place. Catch down the raw inside edge of the neck.

SHAWL COLLAR *(ridged)*

Ridge pattern: K 2 rows, p 2 rows.
Cast on 8 sts.
Pattern 4 rows (for sweaters) *or* pattern until the 8 st band is as long as the front edge of the jacket or

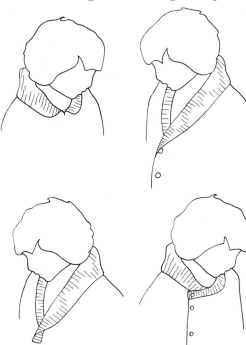

cardigan when slightly stretched (for jackets and cardigans).

Continue in ridge pattern while at the same time increasing one st at beg of next and every alt row until there are 34 sts. Continue straight in ridge pattern until collar measures halfway round the neckline when slightly stretched.

Cast off loosely.

Make a second piece and then sew the 2 pieces together along the cast off edges.

Remember to make buttonholes at regular intervals – yrn, k2 tog – in the front band for jackets and cardigans.

If the simple ribbed band is to be used on a sweater, position the centre seam at the centre back of the neck edge.

For jackets or cardigans, position the cast on edges in line with the front edges of the garment after the button band has been attached.

Place the collar around the outside of the neck edge (inc. edge of collar to neck edge), allowing it to overlap slightly, and sew in place. Catch down the raw inside edge of the neck.

SHAWL COLLAR *(stocking stitch)*

Cast on 90 (C100, CJ120) sts.
St st 4 rows.
Continue in st st shaping the collar as follows:
1st row: P3, yrn, p2 tog, purl to end.
2nd row: K.
3rd row: P.
4th row: K.
5th row: P85 (C95, CJ115) sts, turn.
6th row: K80 (C90, CJ110) sts, turn.
Continue in st st reducing by 5 sts on each row until 25 sts remain.

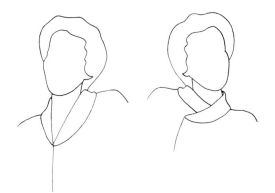

Now increase by 5 sts on each row until all the stitches are being knitted again.
St st 2 rows.
Repeat 1st row.
St st 4 rows.
Cast off loosely.

If the shawl collar is to be used on a sweater, position the short edges at the centre front of the neck edge.

For jackets or cardigans, position the short edges in line with the front edges of the garment after the button band has been attached.

Fold the cast off edge around the outside of the neck edge and catch down. Catch down the cast on edge of the collar on the inside.

OVERLAPPING V *(for V-necks only)*

Choose a rib from the section on stitch patterns.
Cast on 90 sts.
Rib until collar is a suitable length.
(This collar can be made double the length and folded in half to create a more luxurious collar.)
Cast off loosely knitwise.
Place the cast off edge of the collar around the outside of the neck edge, beginning and ending at

the front point of the V. Sew in place. Catch down one short edge of the collar along the outside edge of the V-neck and the other short edge on the underside. Catch down the raw inside edge of the neck.

Lay V insert in place on the outside of the sweater, overlapping the edge slightly. Catch down on the outside and inside. Beginning at the centre back of the sweater, crochet a double chain right round the neck edge.

TRADITIONAL V-NECK
(for V-necks only)

Cast on 90 sts.
1st row: Rib 45, yrn, k1, yrn, rib to end.
2nd row: Rib 46, yrn, p1, yrn, rib to end.
3rd row: Rib 47, yrn, k1, yrn, rib to end.
4th row: Rib 48, yrn, p1, yrn, rib to end.
Work 4 more rows making a st before and after the centre st as above.
Cast off.
Sew the two short ends together and place this seam at the centre back of the neck. Position the point of the V at the centre front of the V-neck, slightly overlapping the edge. Catch down on the outside of the band and on the inside of the neck.

V-INSERT HIGH NECK *(for V-necks only)*

Cast on 2 sts.
Rib 21 rows, inc. one st at beg of each row.
Cast off loosely.

CROCHETED EDGE

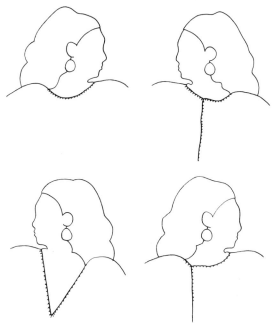

Beginning at the centre back of the sweater, crochet a double chain right round the neck edge.

CONCERTINA RIB *(with loop for sweaters)*

Cast on 90 (C100, CJ120) sts.
Concertina rib pattern:
1st row: K.
2nd row: P.

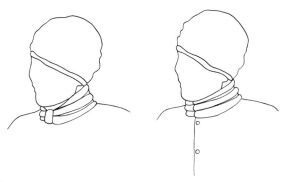

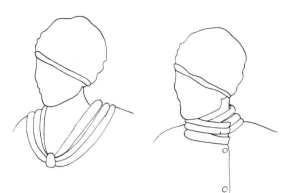

CHEVRON COLLAR *(for sweaters only)*

3rd row: K.
4th row: P.
5th row: P.
6th row: K.
7th row: P.
8th row: K.
Pattern 31 rows.
Next row (wrong side): K.
Next row: K – make a buttonhole (yrn, k2 tog) on the 4th st, or 4th st from the end if for a man's garment, if concertina collar is for a cardigan or jacket.
Next row: P.
Next row: K.
Next row: P.
Cast off loosely knitwise.

If the concertina collar is to be used on a sweater, sew together the short edges and position this seam at the centre back of the neck edge.

For jackets or cardigans, position the short edges in line with the front edges of the garment after the button band has been attached.

Place the cast off edge of the collar around the outside of the neck edge, allowing it to overlap slightly, and sew in place. Catch down the raw inside edge of the neck.
Loop for sweaters:
Cast on 6 sts.
St st 12 rows.
Cast off.
Attach one short edge of the loop on the outside of the centre front of the sweater. Trapping the concertina collar inside the loop, take it over to the inside of the neck and sew down.

Cast on 138 sts.
Work 2 rows in k2, p2 rib, beg alt rows p2.
Next row: Rib 66, p2 tog, k2, p2 tog, rib 66.
Next row: Rib 66, k1, p2, k1, rib 66.
Next row: Rib 65, p2 tog, k2, p2 tog, rib 65.
Next row: Rib 65, k1, p2, k1, rib 65.
Next row: Rib 64, p2 tog, k2, p2 tog, rib 64.
Next row: Rib 64, k1, p2, k1, rib 64.
Continue in this way, dec each side of 2 centre sts on next and every right side row until 90 sts remain.
Next row (right side): K.
Next row: K.
Next row: P.
Next row: K.
Next row: P.
Cast off loosely knitwise.
Place the cast off edge of the collar around the outside of the neck edge, allowing it to overlap slightly, and sew in place. Catch down the raw inside edge of the neck.

POINTED LACE COLLAR

Cast on 90 (C100, CJ120) sts.
St st 6 rows.
K 2 rows.
St st 6 rows.
K 2 rows.

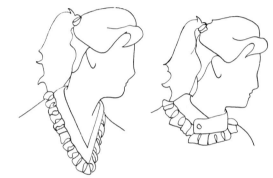

Pointed lace pattern:
1st row: K5, turn.
2nd row: Sl 1, p4, turn.
3rd row: M 1, k3, turn.
4th row: As 2nd row.
5th row: As 3rd row.
6th row: As 2nd row.
7th row: As 3rd row.
8th row: As 2nd row.
9th row: As 3rd row.
10th row: As 2nd row.
11th row: Cast off 9 sts.
12th row: K4, turn.
Repeat from 2nd row to end.

If the pointed lace collar is to be used on a sweater, sew together the short edges and position this seam at the centre back of the neck edge.

For jackets or cardigans, position the short edges in line with the front edges of the garment after the button band has been attached.

Fold the cast on st st band around the neck edge and catch down on the outside and inside.

LOOPY COLLAR

Cast on 91 (C101, CJ121) sts.
St st 6 rows.
K 2 rows.
St st 6 rows.
K 2 rows.
Next row: K3, turn.
Next row: *P3, turn.
Continue on these 3 sts for 13 more rows.
Next row: P3 tog, turn.

Next row: K2 tog, K2, turn *.
Repeat from * to * to last 2 sts, k2 tog, cast off.

If the loopy collar is to used on a sweater, sew together the short edges and position this seam at the centre back of the neck edge.

For jackets or cardigans, position the short edges in line with the front edges of the garment after the button band has been attached.

Fold the cast on st st band around the neck edge and catch down on the outside and inside.

HANDY TIP

If you run short of yarn and can't match the dye lot, intersperse the old and new yarns over about ten rows. This is best done on the back of the garment. Alternatively, use the new yarn for trimmings – collars, cuffs, button bands and making up.

In desperation you might be forced to use a contrasting yarn – so design a Fair Isle pattern and make a feature of it. You'll probably be pleasantly surprised.

SCARF

Cast on 20 sts.
Choose a rib from the section on stitch patterns.
Pattern for as long as you would like the scarf to be.
Cast off.

Fold the scarf in half and position this point at the centre back of the garment, overlapping the edge. Catch down on the outside and inside of the neck edge.

CUFFS

Use needles two sizes smaller than those used for the body and sleeves.

After the cuff has been knitted, increase evenly across the rows to the number of stitches required for the sleeve.

NOTE: The cuff size drawn on the graphs is merely a suggestion. The cuff sizes can be varied according to how loose or tight you would like the cuff to be. However, a minimum of 36 sts is advised.

SINGLE RIB

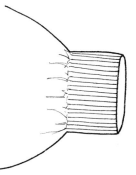

Blouse sleeve: Cast on 40 sts.
Shaped sleeve: Cast on 40 sts.
Shirt sleeve: Cast on 42 sts.
Huge sleeve: Cast on 48 sts.
Raglan sleeve: Cast on one extra st (38 sts).
Every row: K1, p1 to the required length.
Work the increase row and then continue the sleeve, following the chosen pattern.

HANDY TIP

To create a fine contrast edge on the collar, cuffs or welt, use a 'two-strand' method of casting on with two colours of yarn.

Holding the two strands of yarn together, make a slip loop about 25 cm from the ends of the yarn. Slip this double loop on to the needle. Hold the main colour yarn in your right hand, and the contrast yarn in your left hand, and cast on as described.

---

2 × 2 RIB

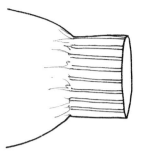

Blouse sleeve: Cast on 40 sts.
Shaped sleeve: Cast on 40 sts.
Shirt sleeve: Cast on 2 less sts (40 sts).
Huge sleeve: Cast on 48 sts.
Raglan sleeve: Cast on one less st (36 sts).
Every row: K2, p2.
Work the increase row and then continue the sleeve following the chosen pattern.

HORIZONTAL 2 ROW STRIPE

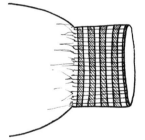

Using 2 colours of yarn, work the cuff alternating the colours every two rows.
Work the increase row and then continue the sleeve following the chosen pattern.

HORIZONTAL 3 ROW STRIPE

Using 3 colours of yarn, work the cuff alternating the colours every row.
Work the increase row and then continue the sleeve following the chosen pattern.

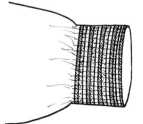

SINGLE RIB VERTICAL STRIPE

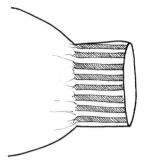

Raglan sleeve: Cast on one stitch less (36 sts).
All other sleeves as shown on the charts.
M = main colour, C = contrast colour.
1st row: *K1M, Cfwd, p1C, Cback*.
2nd row: *Cback, k1C, Cfwd, p1M*.
Work the increase row and then continue the sleeve following the chosen pattern.

CABLED CUFF

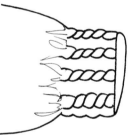

Blouse sleeve: Cast on one extra stitch (41 sts).
Shaped sleeve: Cast on one extra stitch (41 sts).
Shirt sleeve: Cast on one less stitch (41 sts).
Huge sleeve: Cast on 2 less stitches (46 sts).
Raglan sleeve: Cast on one less stitch (36 sts).

1st row: P1, *k4, p1*.
2nd row: K1, *p4, k1*.
3rd row: As 1st row.
4th row: As 2nd row.
5th row: P1, *cable 4 fwd, p1*.
Repeat 2nd, 3rd, 4th and 5th rows twice more.
Work the increase row and then continue the sleeve following the chosen pattern.

MOSS STITCH

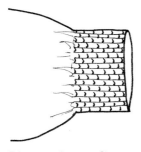

Blouse sleeve: Cast on one extra stitch (41 sts).
Shaped sleeve: Cast on one extra stitch (41 sts).
Shirt sleeve: Cast on one stitch less (41 sts).
Huge sleeve: Cast on one stitch less (47 sts).
Every row: *K1, p1*, k1.
Work the increase row and then continue the sleeve, following the chosen pattern.

FRILLED CUFF

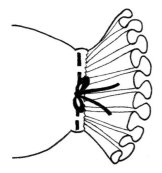

Cast on the number of stitches on the sleeve cuff multiplied by 4 (e.g. raglan sleeve = 37 × 4 = 148 sts; shirt sleeve = 42 × 4 = 168 sts).
1st row: *K3, p1*.
2nd row: *K1, p3*.
3rd row: As 1st row.
4th row: As 2nd row.
5th row: *K2 tog, k1, p1*.
6th row: *K1, p2*.
7th row: *K2, p1*.
8th row: As 6th row.
9th row: *K2 tog, p1*.
10th row: *K1, p1*.
11th row: *K2 tog*.
12th row: P.
13th row: K4, *yrn k2 tog, k6*, yrn k2 tog, k3.

(This row forms a series of holes through which the ribbon is threaded.)
14th Row: Purl all the stitches.
Work the increase row and then continue the sleeve following the chosen pattern.

PICOT-EDGED CUFF

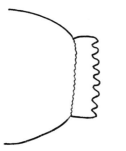

Cast on the number of stitches required for the cuff (e.g. blouse sleeve cuff = 40 sts).
St st 6 rows.
Next row: K1, *yrn, k2 tog*, k1.
Next row: Purl all the stitches.
St st 6 rows.
With right side of work facing, hem edge uppermost, pick up the loose sts of the cast on edge with a spare needle.
Graft the two edges together.
Work the increase row and then continue the sleeve following the chosen pattern.

BROAD TURN BACK

Cast on the same number of stitches as for the bottom of the sleeve (e.g. blouse sleeve = 60 sts).
Pattern a rib, moss stitch or garter stitch to the required length (approx 12 cm (5 in.) for an adult garment), finishing with a right-side row.
Continue the sleeve following the chosen pattern. (When making up, use an invisible seam stitch on the cuff so that when it is turned back no seam is visible.)

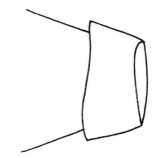

TURNED BACK SPLIT CUFF

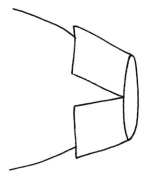

Knit the sleeve, omitting the cuff, and sew up the seam.

With the sleeve right side out and using a smaller sized circular needle, pick up the loose stitches of the cast on edge, beginning halfway from the seam.

Working back and forth across the needle:
st st 3 rows (right sides of sleeve and cuff matching).
K 9 rows, dec 1 st at each end of every row.
Cast off.
Sew in the loose ends and turn back the cuff.

DOLMAN SLEEVE CUFF

Follow any of the patterns above, using the raglan sleeve measurements, and then cast off.
Sew up the side seams.
Place the cuff around the outside of the dolman sleeve and catch down on the outside and the inside.

WELTS

Use needles two sizes smaller than those used for the body and sleeves.

After the welt has been knitted, increase evenly across the rows to the number of stitches required for the body.

NOTE: The welt size drawn on the graphs is merely a suggestion. The welts can be varied according to how loose or tight you would like them to be (e.g. single rib requires a number of stitches divisible by 2 (66, 64, 62, etc.).

The raglan sweater normally has a welt of 65 sts; alter this to 66 sts to fit the single rib pattern. You may also wish to vary the length of the welt.

SINGLE RIB

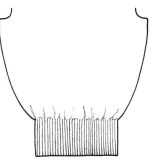

(multiples of 2)
Every row: K1, p1 to the required length.
Work the increase row and then continue the body following the chosen pattern.

2 × 2 RIB

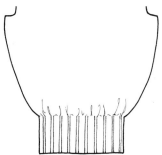

(multiples of 4)
Every row: K2, p2.
Work the increase row and then continue the body following the chosen pattern.

HORIZONTAL 2 ROW STRIPE

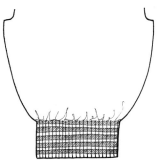

Using 2 colours of yarn, work the welt alternating the colours every two rows.
Work the increase row and then continue the body following the chosen pattern.

HORIZONTAL 3 ROW STRIPE

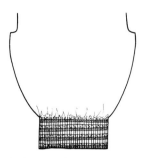

Using 3 colours of yarn, work the welt alternating the colours every row.
Work the increase row and then continue the body following the chosen pattern.

SINGLE RIB VERTICAL STRIPE

(multiples of 2)
M = main colour, C = contrast colour.
1st row: *K1M, Cfwd, p1C, Cback*.
2nd row: *Cback, k1C, Cfwd, p1M*.
Work the increase row and then continue the body following the chosen pattern.

CABLED WELT

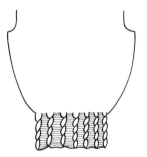

(multiples of 5 + 1)
1st row: P1, *k4, p1*.
2nd row: K1, *p4, k1*.
3rd row: As 1st row.
4th row: As 2nd row.
5th row: P1, *cable 4 fwd, p1*.
Repeat 2nd, 3rd, 4th and 5th rows twice more.
Work the increase row and then continue the body following the chosen pattern.

MOSS STITCH WELT

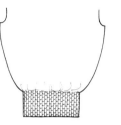

(multiples of 2 + 1)
Every row: *K1, p1*, k1.
Work the increase row and then continue the body following the chosen pattern.

PICOT-EDGED WELT

Cast on the number of stitches required for the welt.
St st 10 rows.
Next row: K1, *yrn, k2 tog*, k1.
Next row: Purl all the stitches.
St st 10 rows.
With right side of work facing, hem edge uppermost, pick up the loose sts of the cast on edge with a spare needle.
Graft the two edges together.
Work the increase row and then continue the body following the chosen pattern.
A drawstring belt can be threaded through the picot-edged welt, but be sure to leave an opening at the side seams for the belt to pass through.

PEPLUM

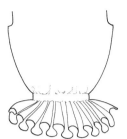

Cast on 240 sts.
1st row: *K3, p1*.
2nd row: *K1, p3*.
3rd row: As 1st row.
4th row: As 2nd row.
5th row: *K2 tog, k1, p1*.
6th row: *K1, p2*.
7th row: *K2, p1*.
8th row: As 6th row.
9th row: *K2 tog, p1*.
10th row: *K1, p1*.
11th row: As 10th row.
12th row: As 10th row.
13th row: *K2 tog*.
14th row: P.
15th row: K3, yrn, k2 tog, *k6, yrn, k2 tog, k3*.
16th row: P.
17th row: K.
18th row: K, increasing evenly to the required number of stitches for the body of the garment.

The 15th row forms a series of eyelet holes through which a ribbon or drawstring belt may be threaded.

TWO-TONE PEPLUM

M = *main colour*, S = *second colour*
Using two strand method, cast on 240 sts.
1st row: *K3M, S fwd, p1S, S back*.
2nd row: *S back k1S, S fwd, p3M*.

3rd row: As 1st row.
4th row: As 2nd row.
5th row: *K2 togM, k1M, S fwd p1S, S back*.
6th row: *S back, k1S, S fwd, p2M*.
7th row: *K2M, S fwd p1S, S back*.
8th row: As 6th row.
9th row: *K2 togM, S fwd p1S, S back*.
10th row: *S back k1S, S fwd, p1M*.
11th row: *K1M, S fwd, p1S, S back*.
12th row: As 10th row.
Continue in main colour only.
13th row: *K2 tog*.
14th row: P.
15th row: K3, yrn, k2 tog, *k6, yrn, k2 tog, k3*.
16th row: P.
17th row: K.
18th row: K, increasing evenly to the required number of stitches for the body of the garment.

The 15th row forms a series of eyelet holes through which a ribbon or drawstring belt may be threaded.

EXTRAS

C = *crossover jacket*
D = *dolman*
RN = *round neck*
V = *V-neck*
R = *raglan*
O = *one-piece*

BUTTONS

Cast on 6sts.
St st 6 rows.
Cast off.
Leave a long thread at the casting on and casting off of each button.
Double one long thread and, using a running stitch, sew around the edges of the square.
Roll up the second long thread and push it into the centre of the button. Pull the first long thread tight and fasten off. Use this thread to sew the button in place.

VERTICAL Y-SHAPED BUTTON BAND *(most suitable for reversible jackets or cardigans)*

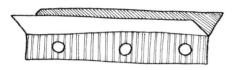

Using the smaller sized needle cast on (CJ90, D66, RN69, V61, R87, O90) sts.
Rib 6 rows.
K 2 rows.
P 1 row.
K 1 row.
Cast off knitwise.
With wrong side of st st facing, cast on edge uppermost and beginning at the right side, pick up (90, 66, 69, 61, 87) sts along the first row above the rib. St st 3 rows beginning with a purl row.
Cast off.

This forms a Y-shaped band. The front edge of the jacket or cardigan is then slipped into the Y and sewn down on both sides.

VERTICAL Y-SHAPED BUTTONHOLE BAND *(most suitable for reversible jackets or cardigans)*

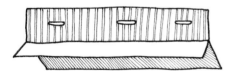

Using the smaller sized needle cast on (CJ90, D66, RN69, V61, R87, O90) sts.
Rib 4 rows.
Buttonhole row: Rib 4 sts, *yrn, k2 tog, rib 8 sts; rep from * as far as possible.
Rib 1 row.
K 2 rows.
P 1 row.
K 1 row.
Cast off knitwise.
With wrong side of stocking stitch facing, cast on edge uppermost and beginning at the right side, pick up (90, 66, 69, 61, 87) sts along the first row above the rib. St st 3 rows beginning with a purl row.
Cast off.

This forms a Y-shaped band. The front edge of the jacket or cardigan is then slipped into the Y and sewn down on both sides.

PLAIN VERTICAL BUTTON BAND

Using the smaller sized needle cast on (CJ90, D66, RN69, V61, R87, O90) sts.
Rib 6 rows.
K 2 rows.
P 1 row.
K 1 row.
Cast off knitwise.
Position the cast on edge of the band along the front edge of the cardigan so that the stocking stitch strip overlaps the edge.
Catch down the band on the outside and inside of the garment.

PLAIN VERTICAL BUTTONHOLE BAND

Using the smaller sized needle cast on (CJ90, D66, RN69, V61, R87, O90) sts.
Rib 4 rows.
Buttonhole row: Rib 4 sts, *yrn, k2 tog, rib 8 sts; rep from * as far as possible.
Rib one row.
K 2 rows.
P 1 row.
K 1 row.
Cast off knitwise
Position the cast on edge of the band along the front edge of the cardigan so that the stocking stitch strip overlaps the edge.
Catch down the band on the outside and inside of the garment.

HORIZONTAL BUTTON BAND

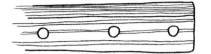

Using the smaller sized needle cast on 12 sts.
1st row: (K1, p1) 4 times, k4.
2nd row: P4, (k1, p1) 4 times.
These two rows form the pattern for the button band. Continue until when slightly stretched the band is the same length as the front edge of the jacket.
Lay the stocking stitch edge on top of the front edge of the jacket and sew in place on back and front.

HORIZONTAL BUTTONHOLE BAND

Using the smaller sized needle cast on 11 sts.
1st row: K4, p1, rib 6 sts.
2nd row: Rib 6 sts, k1, p4.
Repeat these two rows twice.
Buttonhole row: K4, p1, k1, p1, yrn, k2 tog, k1, p1.
Next row: As 2nd row.
Continue the buttonhole band, forming a button-hole in every 10th row until when slightly stretched the band is the same length as the front edge of the jacket.
Sew in place in the same way as the horizontal button band.

ARMHOLE BANDS

Cast on (CJ120, RN100, V100, R108, O120) sts.
Rib 12 rows.
Cast off.
Sew short ends of band together then fold around the armhole and sew in place.

RIBBED BELT

Cast on 12 sts.
Single rib to the required length.
Cast off.

PLAITED BELT

Make three lengths of st st (10 sts) one and a half times longer than the required belt. Instead of casting off each length, graft the three lengths together and then cast off.

Plait the three lengths and then sew in the loose ends, securing the end of the plait.

DRAWSTRING BELT

Using three strands of mohair together, single crochet to the required length.

SIDE SEAM POCKET
(not suitable for one-piece jacket)

When the front(s) and back of the garment have been knitted, sew 10 cm (4 in.) of the side seams beginning at the welt.

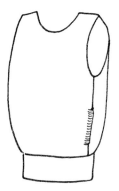

Holding the back of the garment with right side facing, edge uppermost, pick up 25 sts along the edge.

St st 50 rows beginning with a purl row.

Fold the pocket strip in half.

Graft these 25 sts on to the front pocket edge.

Rib 4 rows.

Cast off loosely.

Sew the inside edges of the pocket.

Catch down the short ends of the ribbed pocket band.

PATCH POCKETS

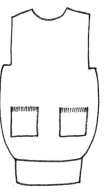

Cast on 24 sts.

St st 24 rows.

Rib 6 rows.

Cast off and sew in place.

VERTICAL POCKET

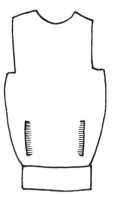

* Look at the graph chart of your chosen garment and decide where you would like the pocket(s) to

be. Draw a vertical line 30 rows deep, beginning immediately above the increase row above the welt.

After you have knitted the welt and the increase row, work only as far as the vertical line for 30 rows. Hold these sts on a spare needle and then work 30 rows of the second section of the pattern. (You will have to repeat this a third time if you decide to include two pockets on the one-piece jacket, as the body is made in one piece.) You will now have two (or three) separate pieces of knitting stemming from the welt.
Put all the stitches back on to one needle and work right across the row.
Continue on these stitches in the usual way, shaping the armholes and neck as appropriate. **

To complete the pocket:

Holding the back of the garment with right side facing, edge uppermost, pick up 25 sts along the edge.
St st 50 rows beginning with a purl row.
Fold the pocket strip in half.
Graft these 25 sts on to the front pocket edge.
Rib 4 rows.
Cast off loosely.
Sew the inside edges of the pocket.
Catch down the short ends of the ribbed pocket band.

For reversible one-piece jacket:

Follow the instructions above from * to ** on the inner or outer side of the garment only.

To complete the pocket:

Catch down the back and upper edges of the pocket to the reversible side of the garment.
Pick up 25 sts along the front pocket edge.
Rib 4 rows.
Cast off loosely.
Catch down the short ends of this ribbed pocket band.

AFTERTHOUGHT POCKET

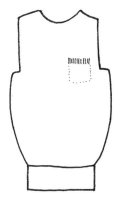

Having made up your sweater, you might decide it would have been nice to have added a pocket.

Decide where you would like the pocket to be and mark the centre of the opening with a pin. Snip the stitch at this point and carefully unravel the stitches to right and left for 5 cm (2 in.), making an opening of 10 cm (4 in.).
Pick up the stitches on the bottom row and leave on a stitch holder.
Pick up the stitches on the top row and work 40 rows st st.
Fold the pocket in half and, keeping the pocket on the inside of the garment, graft the pocket stitches together with the stitches on the stitch holder.
Rib 4 rows.
Cast off.
Sew up the sides of the pocket and secure the ribbed edge.
Sew in all loose ends.

EPAULETTES

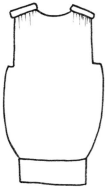

Cast on 8 sts.
St st a strip which matches the distance from the neck to the shoulder edge.
Cast off.

The epaulette can be used (**a**) as a decoration, sewn in place at the neck and shoulder edge and adorned with a button; or (**b**) to draw in overlarge shoulders and so create a smaller sized coat from a large sized pattern (see 'Flight' on page 135).

SHOULDER PADS

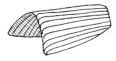

Cast on 12 sts.
St st 8 rows.
Cast off 1 st at beginning of next 8 rows.
Cast on 1 st at beginning of next 8 rows.
St st 8 rows.
Cast off.
Fold the shoulder pad in half. Stuff with scraps of mohair and sew up the edges.
Sew the straight edge of the pad along the shoulder edge on the inside of the sweater. Catch the pointed edge down towards the neck edge.

LINING A GARMENT WITH MATERIAL (*most suitable for jackets and cardigans*)

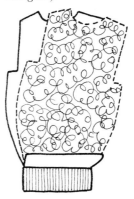

Before making up the garment:
With the wrong side of the knitting facing you, cast on edge uppermost, and beginning at the right-hand side of the body or cuff, pick up the sts from the increase row of each pattern piece (e.g. 160 sts on the one-piece jacket body, or 80 sts on the back of the crossover jacket and 58 sts on the fronts).
St st 6 rows.
Cast off.
This forms a slot into which the lining is slipped and the edging is then sewn down on top of the lining.
Next:
Lay each piece out flat on top of the lining material to act as a pattern. Cut out the shapes, allowing a 2 cm ($\frac{3}{4}$ in.) seam allowance around each piece (on non-stretch materials allow a 4 cm [$1\frac{1}{2}$ in.] seam allowance).

Sew the side seams and the shoulder seams of the lining. If applicable, sew the sleeve seams and sew the seams in place.

With wrong sides of garment and lining facing, pin the lining in place on the inside of the garment. Pin around the armholes first, then around the neck, and finally, slip the bottom of the lining into the welt edging. (With non-stretch material you will have to gather the extra material evenly into the slot formed by the edging.) Pin in place.

Do the same with the cuffs.

Oversew the welt edging on to the lining.

Oversew the cuff edging on to the lining.

Fold under the raw edge of the neck lining and oversew around the neck edge.

Sew the collar in place.

TASSLES

Cut mohair into 60 cm (24 in.) lengths. Fold a length in half twice (4 strands). Fold in half again and, using a crochet hook and working from bottom to top on the right side of the garment, draw the centre fold through the garment to form a loop.

Twist the crochet hook around the threads and draw them all through the loop. Pull to secure.

KNITTING TRIANGLES OR RECTANGLES ON TO THE FINISHED GARMENT

Decide how big and in what position you would like your shapes to be.

Pick up a number of stitches (depending on the width of your triangle or rectangle) on the right side of the garment.

For triangles:

St st 2 rows.

Dec 1 st at beg of all following rows until one st remains. Draw the yarn through the last stitch and either (**a**) attach a bead to the bottom of the triangle; or (**b**) secure the bottom of the triangle to the garment.

For rectangles:

St st to the required length. Cast off and either (**a**) sew in the loose end; or (**b**) secure the bottom of the rectangle to the garment.

· 4 ·

COMBINATIONS

ROUND NECK

(**a**) *Sweater*
- blouse sleeve
- overlay slit collar
- cuffs and welt in single rib
- two-tone diagonal stripe pattern on body and sleeves

(**b**) *Tunic*
- extended pattern to tunic length
- shaped sleeve
- polo collar
- cuffs and welt in single rib
- beaded all over

(**c**) *Cardigan*
- shaped sleeve
- swollen rib collar
- horizontal button bands
- single rib cuffs
- garter stitch to armhole shaping, then stocking stitch in Fair Isle design

(**d**) *Cardigan*
- blouse sleeve
- detachable yoke
- horizontal 2 row striped cuffs
- flecked mohair yarn

V-NECKS

(**a**) *Sweater*
- shirt sleeve gathered into puff at shoulder
- V-insert high neck collar
- cuffs and welt in single rib
- bobbles knitted in at random

(**b**) *Sweater*
- shaped sleeve
- overlapping V-collar
- cabled cuff
- welt in cable rib
- knitted strips attached at random

(**c**) *Waistcoat*
- armbands
- vertical button bands
- monogram knitted in or Swiss darned

(**d**) *Gilet*
- made two sizes larger and pleated across the shoulders
- armbands
- traditional V-neck

CROSSOVER JACKET

(**a**) *Cardigan*
- shaped sleeve edged in contrast colour, no cuffs
- shawl collar edged in contrast colour
- picot edged welt
- front edges backed with petersham ribbon, popper fastenings
- flecked yarn
- ribbed belt

(**b**) *Jacket*
- shirt sleeve gathered into puff at shoulders
- buttoned collar
- single rib cuff trimmed with fur
- picot-edged welt
- vertical button bands

(**c**) *Coat*
- pattern extended to coat length
- blouse sleeve
- extra-long polo collar in moss stitch
- moss stitch cuffs and welt
- front edges bound in ribbon with only one button at neck

(**d**) *Coat*
- pattern extended to coat length
- huge sleeves pleated at shoulders and tucked under armbands
- broad turned-back cuffs
- vertical button bands, three buttonholes
- mock double-breasted knitted buttons
- short buttoned collar made with 90 sts fastening centre front
- bouclé mohair

ONE-PIECE JACKET

(**a**) *Heavyweight gilet*
- armbands
- large polo collar in 2 × 2 rib
- horizontal button band extending right up to front edge of polo collar
- cabled fronts on one side, plain reverse
- welt in 2 × 2 rib

(**b**) *Waistcoat*
- armbands, swollen rib collar and welt in 2 × 2 rib
- contrast colour reverse
- no button bands (invisible seam to join fronts)
- contrast coloured beaded knitting across shoulder
- side pocket on one side, afterthought pocket on the other

(**c**) *Jacket*
- huge sleeves
- cuffs and welt in single rib
- shawl collar (stocking stitch)
- Fair Isle pattern on one side, plain colour reverse
- vertical Y-shaped button bands

(**d**) *Jacket*
- reduced length pattern
- no collar, cuffs or welt
- huge sleeves bound at cuff with ribbon
- lined throughout with material
- bound in ribbon round neck, down fronts and along hem

RAGLAN

(**a**) *Sweater*
- raglan sleeves
- peplum and single rib welt
- polo collar and cuffs in single rib
- sequins and beads sewn on sleeve

(**b**) *Coat*
- pattern extended to coat length
- raglan sleeves
- broad turn-back cuff
- horizontal button bands
- double-width ribbed belt

(**c**) *Sweater*
- raglan sleeves
- simple ribbed band collar
- single rib cuffs and welt
- Fair Isle pattern across chest and upper arms

(**d**) *Sweater*
- raglan sleeves
- single rib vertical-striped cuffs, welt and collar
- front slit collar
- two-coloured Fair Isle pattern all over

DOLMAN

(**a**) *Sweater*
- 2 × 2 rib cuffs and welt (cuffs attached afterwards)
- scarf collar
- Fair Isle pattern along sleeves

(**b**) *Sweater*
- cowl-collared hood
- single rib cuffs and welt
- multi-coloured triangles attached at random

(**c**) *Sweater*
- buttoned collar
- 2 × 2 rib cuffs and welt
- material patches appliquéd at random

(**d**) *Sweater*
- double-width scarf collar
- single rib cuffs and welt
- off-centre front cable panel

· 5 ·

KNITTING TECHNIQUES

CASTING ON

TWO-STRAND METHOD

Measure a length of yarn three times the length of the final cast on edge. Make a slip loop and slip it on to a needle. Hold the needle and the yarn from the ball in the right hand, the short thread in the left hand.

*Holding the left thread taut across the left palm, loop the left thread around the left thumb.

Insert the needle into the front of the loop, pass the right thread around the needle and knit to form a stitch.

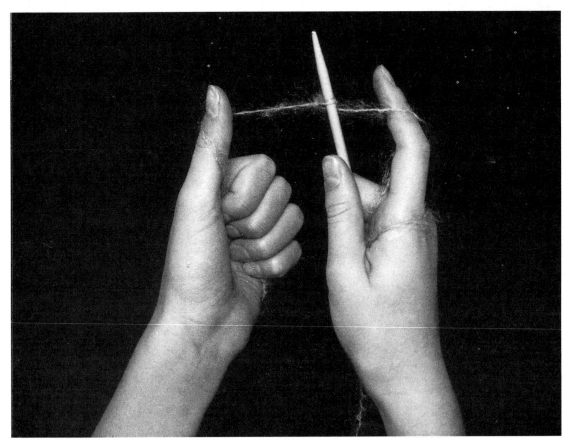

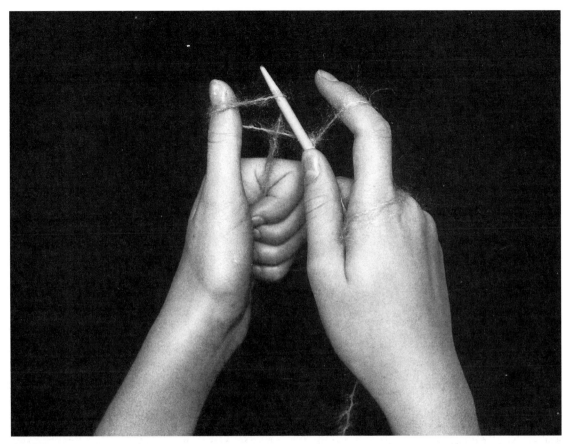

Pull both threads firmly.**
Repeat from * to ** to the required number of
stitches.

CONTINENTAL TWO-STRAND
METHOD

Measure a length of yarn three times the length of
the final cast on edge. Holding two needles
together, make a slip loop and slip it on to the two
needles. Hold the needles and the yarn from the
ball in the right hand, the short thread across the
left palm with the palm facing your body.
*Holding the left thread taut with the last three
fingers, slip the thumb and forefinger under the
thread.

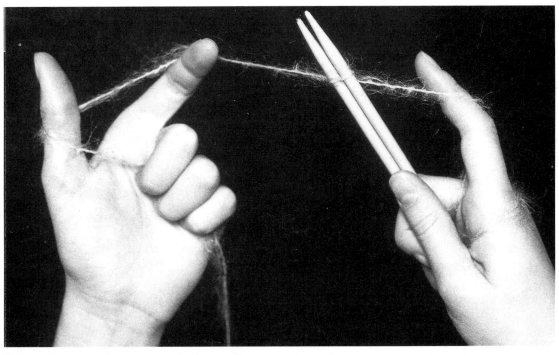

Rotate these two fingers towards the needles so that the thumb lies next to the needles.

Insert the needles into the front of the loop that has been formed, pick up the back of the loop and bring it forward.

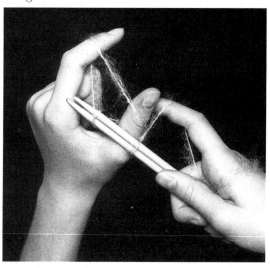

Take the right thread round the needle and knit to form a stitch.**

Repeat from * to ** to the required number of stitches, then withdraw one of the needles and continue knitting in the usual way.

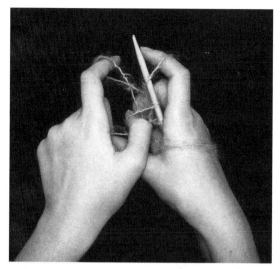

Using two needles instead of one creates a more elastic edge and makes it much easier to knit the first row.

FRENCH TWO-NEEDLE METHOD

Make a slip loop about 25 cm (10 in.) from the end of the yarn. Slip it on to the left needle and pull it taut.

*Holding the yarn in the right hand, insert the right needle into the loop. Pass the thread round the right needle (as for ordinary knitting), draw through a loop and slip it onto the left needle to form a new stitch.**

Repeat from * to ** to the required number of stitches.

ENGLISH TWO-NEEDLE METHOD

Make a slip loop about 25 cm (10in.) from the end of the yarn. Slip it on to the left needle and pull it taut.

Holding the yarn in the right hand, insert the right needle into the loop. Pass the thread round the right needle (as for ordinary knitting), draw through a loop and slip it on to the left needle to form a second stitch.

*Insert the needle into the space between the last two stitches.

Pass the thread round the right needle, draw through a loop and slip it on to the left needle to form a new stitch.**

Repeat from * to ** to the required number of stitches.

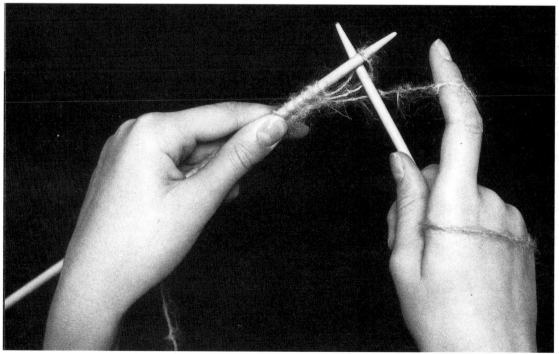

CASTING OFF

SIMPLE CAST OFF

Take a needle one size larger than those used for the garment and use this as the right-hand needle (this helps to prevent creating too tight a cast-off edge). Knit two stitches. Pass the first stitch over the second stitch and off the needle. Knit a third stitch and pass the second stitch over it and off the needle.

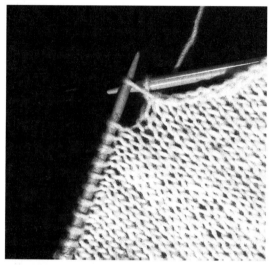

Continue in this way to the required number of cast off stitches.
When working purl or rib patterns the stitches can be worked according to the pattern and cast off in the same way.

SUSPENDED CAST OFF

(This method of casting off also helps to prevent creating too tight an edge.)

Knit two stitches. Insert the left-hand needle through the front of the first stitch and pass it over the second stitch on to the left-hand needle. Keeping this stitch on the left-hand needle, knit the third stitch and only allow the cast-off stitch to slip off the needle when the new stitch is formed. Continue casting off in this way, holding on to the cast off stitch until a new stitch is formed.

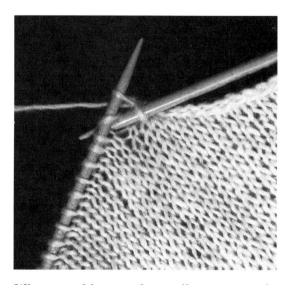

When working purl or rib patterns the stitches can be worked according to the pattern and cast off in the same way.

INCREASING

BAR INCREASE

Knit into the front of the stitch but before slipping the stitch off the needle knit again into the back of the stitch.
Slip the 2 sts on to the right-hand needle.
With a purl stitch, purl into the front of the stitch, and without slipping the stitch from the needle take the yarn back between the needles and knit into the back of the stitch.

This method of increasing produces a small 'bar' which makes it easy to count how many increases have been worked. To achieve a symetrical pattern in a garment it is necessary to work a 'bar' increase one stitch closer to the edge of the right-hand side of the garment than to the left, e.g. k2, inc 1 in the *3rd st*, k to last 4 sts, inc 1 in the *4th st from the end*, k3.

Alternatively, the increases can be made on alternate rows, e.g.

1st row: K2, inc 1, pattern to end.
2nd row: P2, inc 1, pattern to end.

INVISIBLE INCREASE

Insert the right-hand needle from front to back through the top of the stitch below the next one to be knitted. Pass the thread round the right-hand needle and knit this stitch in the usual way.

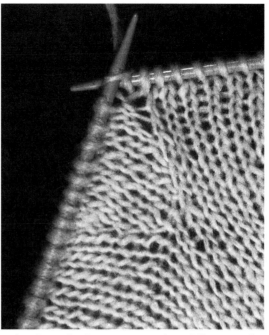

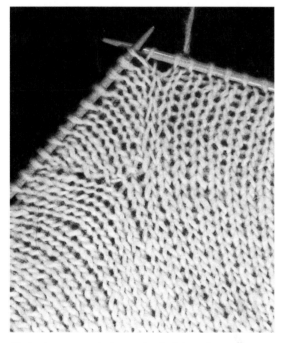

Knit the next stitch on the left-hand needle.
With a purl stitch, insert the right-hand needle from back to front through the top of the stitch below the next one to be knitted. Pass the thread round the right-hand needle and purl this stitch in the usual way.

This method of increasing is suitable for large areas of increasing, e.g. on the first row above the welt where the increase row gives fullness to the garment.

INSET INCREASE

Insert the left-hand needle from front to back through the horizontal thread lying between the two stitches. Knit into the back of this thread.

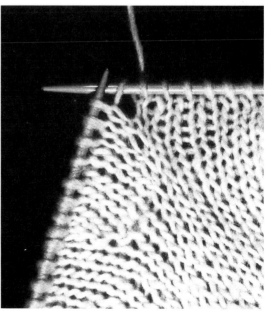

With a purl stitch, insert the left-hand needle from back to front through the horizontal thread lying between the two stitches. Purl into the front of this thread.

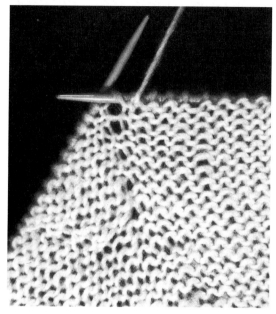

To achieve a symmetrical pattern, make an increase at the same point from both edges, e.g. k2, inc 1, k to last 2 sts, inc one, k2.

YRN

In a knit row, bring the yarn forward through the needles.

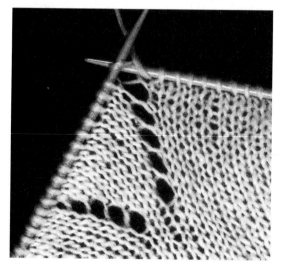

Insert the right needle from front to back into the next stitch and knit this stitch in the usual way. On the next row knit (or purl) the yarn-round stitch in the usual way.

In a purl row, take the yarn over the top of the right-hand needle and round between the needles to the front.

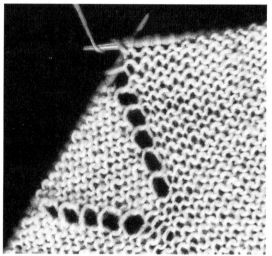

Purl the next stitch in the usual way. On the next row purl (or knit) the yarn-round stitch in the usual way.

DECREASING

WORKING ON THE RIGHT SIDE OF THE GARMENT

Slanting to the left:
Slip a stitch (purlwise), knit the next stitch and then pass the slipped stitch over this knitted stitch and off the needle.

Slanting to the right:
Knit two stitches together from left to right through the fronts of the stitches.

WORKING ON THE WRONG SIDE OF THE GARMENT

Slanting to the left on the plain side of the garment:
Purl a stitch, put it back on to the left-hand needle. Slip the second stitch on the left-hand needle over this stitch from left to right and off the needle.

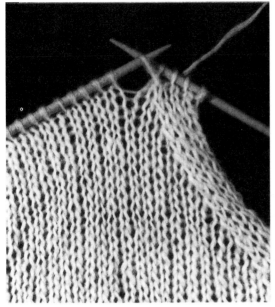

Put the stitch back on to the right-hand needle.
Slanting to the right on the plain side of the garment:
Purl two stitches together.

GRAFTING

GRAFTING BY SEWING

(a) Two pieces of stocking stitch:

Lay the two pieces to be grafted right sides uppermost, with the stitches facing each other. Slip one stitch at a time off the needles and sew the two pieces together as shown.

(b) Two pieces of reverse stocking stitch:

Lay the pieces to be grafted right sides uppermost, with the stitches facing each other. Slip one stitch at a time off the needles and sew them together as shown.

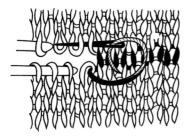

(c) Two pieces of garter stitch:

Before grafting these two pieces together, make sure that one piece finishes with a knit row, the other with a purl row.

Lay the pieces right sides uppermost with the stitches facing each other. Slip one stitch at a time off the needles and sew them together.

(d) Two pieces of 2 × 2 rib:

Before grafting these two pieces together, make sure that the opposite ribs match – knit to knit, purl to purl, and in the number of stitches.

Lay the pieces right sides uppermost with the stitches facing each other. Slip one stitch at a time off the needles and sew them together as shown.

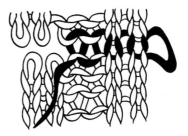

GRAFTING BY KNITTING

Keeping the two pieces to be grafted on the needles and with right sides facing, hold them together in the left hand.

Using a needle one size larger (and double-pointed if possible) in the right hand, slip one stitch (purlwise) from the front needle, and one stitch (purlwise) from the back needle, alternately, as far as required.

Next row: K2 tog all along this row.
Next row: Cast off.

STRANDING, WEAVING AND CROSSING

These three techniques are used when knitting with more than one colour of yarn. They prevent holes from appearing and keep the back of the work neat.

STRANDING

This method should be used when working Fair Isle patterns, narrow stripes, and other patterns which use small multiples of stitches and only two colours. Yarn should not be stranded over more than five stitches.

Working on the right side:
Keep both colours at the back of the work. Work the required number of stitches with colour A and then let it fall to the back. Pick up colour B and work the required number of stitches with this yarn before letting it fall to the back. When purling stitches, the yarn is brought forward in the usual way, but is taken to the back before picking up the second colour.

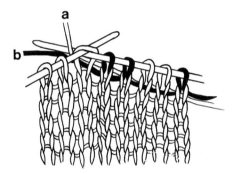

Working on the wrong side:
Keep both colours at the front of the work. Work the required number of stitches with colour A and then let it fall to the front. Pick up colour B and work the required number of stitches with this yarn before letting it fall to the front. When the stitches are being knitted the yarn is taken back to knit the stitch, and brought forward again before picking up the second colour.

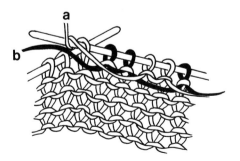

If the yarns are pulled too tightly the knitting will look puckered. When stranding has been worked correctly the yarns running across the back of the knitting will look even and be the same tension as the knitting.

WEAVING

This method should be used with large pattern repeats, where the yarn has to be carried over more than five stitches, and for patterns using more than two colours. Because the 'carried' thread is held securely at the back of the knitting it prevents it from being caught or snagged. This is particularly important on the inside of sleeves.

Working on the right side:
Keep the yarns at the back of the work with the working yarn A in your right hand, and yarn B in your left hand. Hold up yarn B and knit one stitch with yarn A round the back of yarn B.

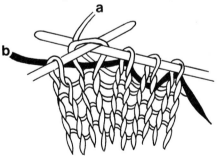

Hold down yarn B and knit one stitch with yarn A.

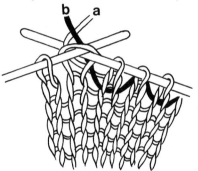

Working on the wrong side:
Keep the yarns at the front of the work with yarn A in your right hand, and yarn B in your left hand.

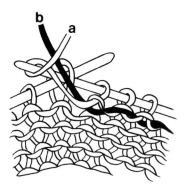

Hold up yarn B and purl one stitch with yarn A
round the front of yarn B.
Hold down yarn B and purl one stitch with yarn A.

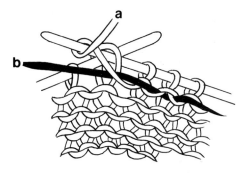

CROSSING

This method is used when working large, separate
motifs, or broad vertical or horizontal stripes,
where it is not necessary to carry the second colour
along the row. It prevents a hole forming where
the two colours meet.

Take the yarn you used for the last stitch across to
the left. Bring the second yarn under the first yarn
and continue to knit (or purl).

BEADED KNITTING

Before knitting, the beads have to be threaded on
to the yarn. Beads are sometimes sold on a length
of string and can be directly transferred on to the
yarn.

If you want to create a multi-coloured pattern
with beads, first draw out your pattern on squared
paper and then, working from the top of the
pattern, thread the beads in the order they will be
knitted.

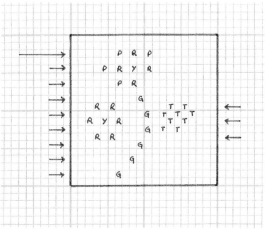

The beads in the chart would be threaded in the
following order:

P R P P R Y R P R G T T R R G T T T T T R Y R G T T R R
G G G

(If you are planning to make an all-over beaded
garment, the beads should only be knitted on
alternate rows and never on the first or last stitch,
as this results in curling.)

Method 1: **PLACING A BEAD AT THE CENTRE OF AN EVEN NUMBER OF STITCHES**

(Since the bead will drop slightly, it should be charted and knitted on the row above where it will eventually lie – see 'diamond bead' pattern.)

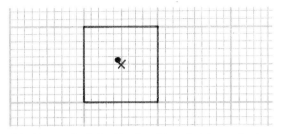

Working on the right side of stocking stitch (e.g. placing the bead at the centre of 4 sts):
K2, y fwd, push the bead up close to the needle, p1, y back, continue to knit.
Working on the wrong side of stocking stitch (e.g. placing the bead at the centre of 4 sts):
P2, y back, push the bead up close to the needle, k1, y fwd, continue to purl.

Method 2: **PLACING A BEAD AT THE CENTRE OF AN ODD NUMBER OF STITCHES**

(This beaded stitch is charted and knitted at the point where it will lie.)

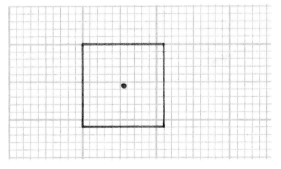

Working on the right side of stocking stitch (e.g. placing the bead at the centre of 5 sts):
K2, y fwd, sl 1 purlwise and push the bead up close to the needle, y back and continue to knit.
Working on the wrong side of stocking stitch (e.g. placing the bead at the centre of 5 sts):
P2, y back, sl 1 purlwise and push the bead up close to the needle, y fwd and continue to purl.

SWISS DARNING

Swiss darning is a simple way of adding small patterns, pictures, letters and numbers. It produces a slightly raised effect over the knitted stitches. If your design requires many small amounts of different coloured yarns, they can get tangled up when knitted into the garment. Swiss darning avoids this tangle and also avoids the risk of holes forming between the different motifs.

WORKING HORIZONTALLY

Secure the yarn at the back of the knitting and bring it out at the base of the stitch you want to cover (a). Insert the needle under the two strands of the stitch above (b) and pull it through. Insert the needle back through (a) and bring it out at the base of the next stitch you want to cover (c).

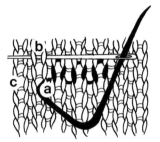

WORKING VERTICALLY

Secure the yarn at the back of the knitting and bring it out at the base of the stitch you want to cover (a). Insert the needle under the two strands of the stitch above (b) and pull it through.

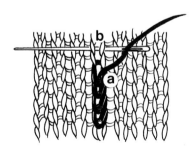

Insert the needle under the head of the darned stitch below the one you are working (c) and pull it through at the base of the next stitch you want to cover.

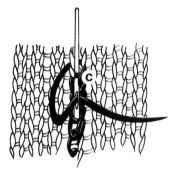

(For the first stitch, you will have to insert the needle under the head of the knitted stitch below the one you are working.)

EMBROIDERY

BACK STITCH

Bring the thread through at (a). Make a small backwards stitch through (b) and bring the thread through at (c). Make sure the distances a–b and a–c are the same.

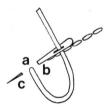

CHAIN STITCH

Bring the thread out at (a) and hold it down with your left thumb. Insert the needle back through (a) and bring the point out a short distance away. Keep the working thread under the point of the needle and pull the thread through.

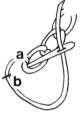

SATIN STITCH

Take care not to pull the stitches too tightly; work straight stitches closely together across the shape.

If chain stitch is first worked over the shape to form a padding, the satin stitch will have a raised effect. Do not make the stitches too long, as they are likely to catch.

BUTTONHOLE STITCH

Bring the thread through at (a). Insert the needle at (b) and bring the point back out at (c). Keeping the working thread under the point of the needle, pull the needle through.

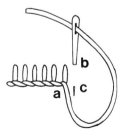

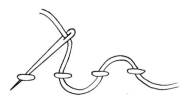

LACED RUNNING STITCH

Make a series of running stitches. Lace or whip these with a contrasting thread, making sure not to pick up any of the knitting.

CROCHET

SINGLE CHAIN

Make a slip loop and thread it on to a crochet hook. Hold the hook in your right hand and the yarn in your left. Twist the hook under and then over the yarn.

Draw the yarn through to form a link.

DOUBLE CROCHET

Make a chain. Insert the hook back into the second link from the hook.

Catch the yarn with the hook and draw it through the chain. Twist the yarn round the hook and draw it through the two loops on the hook.

Continue to work double crochets into the next and following links to the end of the row.

Next and following rows: Make a link and turn. Continue by inserting the hook into the space below the stitches in the previous row.

TREBLE CROCHET

Make a chain. Twist the hook round the yarn and then insert it into the fifth link from the hook. Twist the hook round the yarn again and draw through a loop.

Twist the hook round the yarn again and draw the yarn through the first two loops on the hook.

Twist the hook round the yarn again and draw the yarn through the remaining two loops.

Continue making treble crochets along the chain, then turn.

Make three links and then work the treble crochets into the space below the stitches in the previous row.

HANDY TIP

If you find that the yarn you need is at the wrong side of the garment, when working a Fair Isle or picture design, slip the stitches on to a circular needle. You can then begin knitting again from the opposite side.

MAKING UP

BACKSTITCH SEAM

This seam is most suitable for mohair knitting, as it produces a strong, firm seam.

Lay the pieces to be joined together on a flat surface, with right sides facing. Pin them in place, making sure to match patterns, rows and stitches. Working 5 mm ($\frac{1}{4}$ in.) from the edge of the knitting, backstitch along the seam.

EDGE TO EDGE SEAM

This seam is useful on lightweight knits and garments with delicate stitch patterns. It makes no ridge and is almost invisible.

Lay the pieces to be joined together on a flat surface. Carefully match the patterns stitch for stitch and row for row, with the 'heads' of the stitches touching. Work back and forth, sewing into the heads of the stitches.

ATTACHING COLLARS

If the collar is to be attached to a sweater, sew down the short edge of the collar to make a circle.

Lay the cast off edge of the collar in place on the outside of the garment about 5 cm (2 in.) from the neck edge, balancing its position from the centre back.
Catch it down through each stitch of the edge of the collar.

Catch down the raw inside edge to strengthen the seam and neaten the edge.

ATTACHING CUFFS

This normally applies only to dolman cuffs, which can be attached in the same way as collars.

They can also be grafted on to the sleeves:
Pick up the same number of stitches as there are on the cuff along the edge of the sleeve.
Keeping the cuff and sleeve on their needles, hold them together with right sides facing and join them by using the knitting method of grafting.

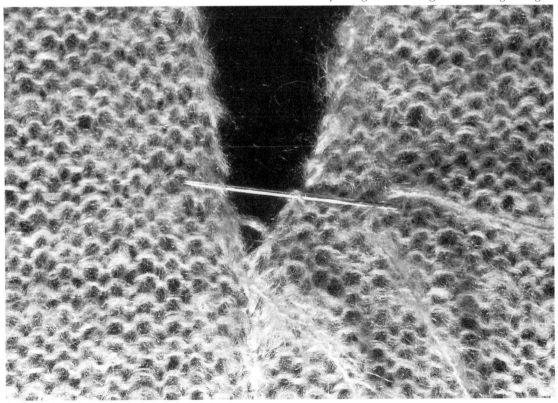

WASHING AND DRYING

Mohair can be dry-cleaned or washed.

WASHING

As with wool, care in washing and drying is necessary to prevent your garment from shrinking and to keep it soft and luxurious.

Hand wash your mohair garment in plenty of warm water, using a liquid detergent. Squeeze it gently and do not rub. Do not leave the garment to soak. Rinse it in plenty of warm water, making sure that the temperature is the same as the washing water. When the water is clear, you can add fabric conditioner to the final rinse.

Squeeze out as much water as possible before rolling the garment in a clean towel and squeezing out any further water. You may need more than one towel.

You can also wash mohair in a washing machine that has a wool wash program. Spinning the garment is an excellent way of taking out the maximum amount of water.

Lay the mohair garment out on a dry towel away from direct sunlight and reshape it.

To restore the fluffiness of mohair, either use a soft brush to draw up the fibres, or blow warm air from a hairdryer through from the back of the garment (but be careful not to block the air passage of the dryer).

Do not iron mohair, as ironing flattens the fibres.

When the garment is dry, fold the sleeves across the front of the chest and then fold the welt up to the shoulder line. Store your mohair garment in a drawer, never on a hanger, as it may pull out of shape.

DRY-CLEANING

This is of course a very good way of caring for clothes, but if you want to add extras to your garment (beads, buttons, feathers, ribbons, etc.), make a small test strip including a few of these extras and ask your dry-cleaner to clean it before you begin your garment, just to establish whether any difficulties are likely.

1. 'Jade'

2. 'Siberia'

3. 'Diamonds'

4. 'Lesotho Blue'

5. 'Whisper'

DESIGN TECHNIQUES

USING COLOUR

SYMBOLS TO SHOW COLOUR

The easiest way to design in colour is by using crayons or felt pens (see the jacket of this book). However, if you do not have a plentiful supply, use symbols on your graph paper to denote colour or stitch patterns.

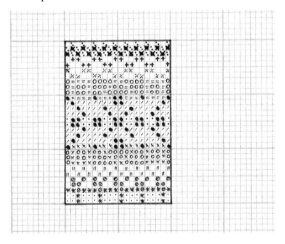

BLOCKING

Outline the motif and colour it with a crayon or felt pen, or simply write in the selected colour.

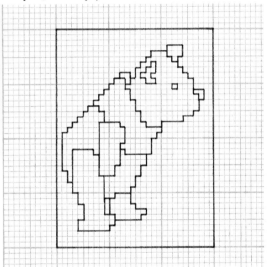

SYMBOLS AND BLOCKING COMBINED

Use a combination of the last two methods where your design includes stitch patterns and colour patterns together.

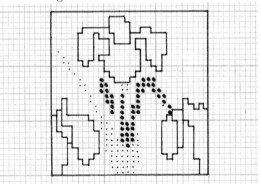

85

PLANNING A COLOUR DESIGN

Plan your design so that there are always two rows of pattern before you reintroduce a colour.

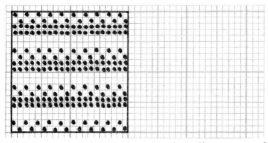

This may not be so obvious in a heavily patterned design, but the principle is still the same.

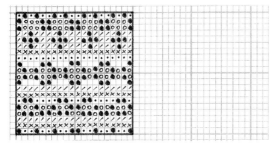

Planning your design in this way avoids having to break off the yarn at one side of the garment in order to reintroduce it at the other side, saving endless sewing-in of loose threads.

CENTRING DESIGNS

When planning a Fair Isle or repeated design, start from the centre of the pattern and work out to the sides. This is particularly important with large designs so as not to create a lopsided effect.

MULTI-COLOURED REPEATED PATTERNS

Try to use only two colours per row and so cut down the tangle. Many variations can be obtained on this two-colour row principle.

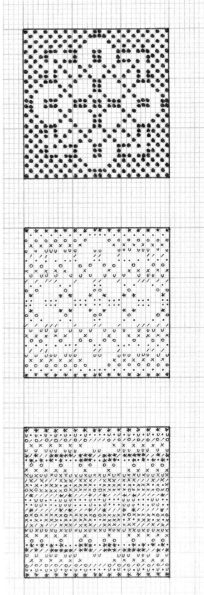

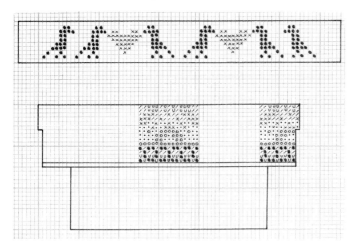

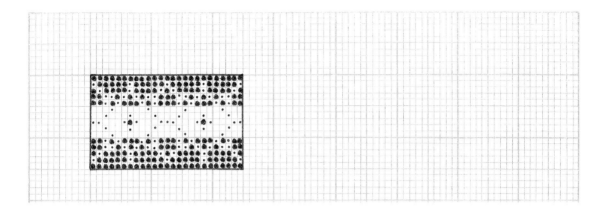

However, to obtain a symmetrical effect on an odd-numbered pattern you will either have to break the yarn at one side and reintroduce it, or you can work three colours on one row to bring the yarns to the right side.

PICTURE SWEATERS

Since most stitches are rectangular in shape and graph paper is square, it is difficult to design a truly representative picture. Pictures are easier to create, therefore, if they are stylized.

Draw or trace a picture on to your pattern.

Outline the edges of the stitches around the motifs.

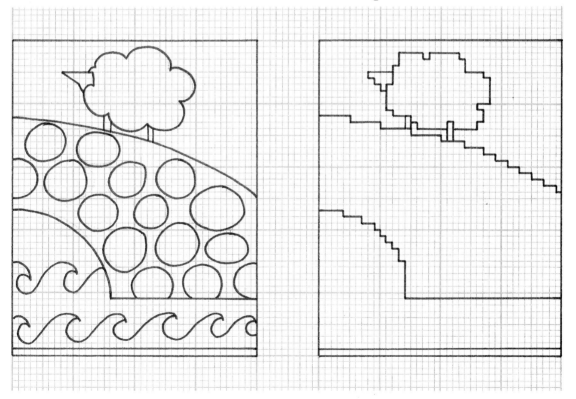

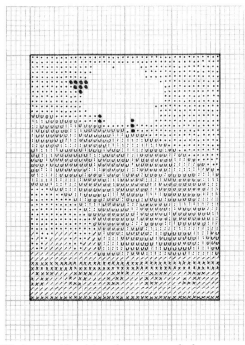

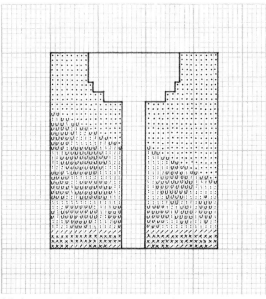

Make sure the side seams match.

First design the front(s) and back of your garment. Then, beginning at the point of underarm shaping, work up and down the sleeve, matching this design.

Fill the motifs with colour or symbols.

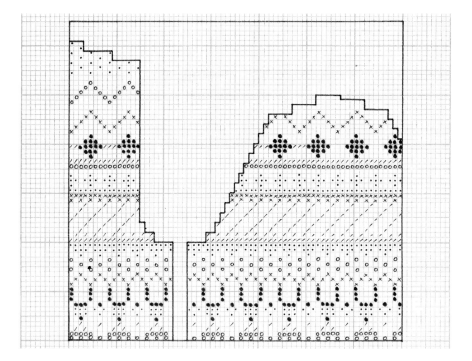

Where symmetry is required, plan one half of the design and then 'mirror-image' the second half.

ISOLATED MOTIFS

When your design includes small, isolated motifs (as in 'Flight', page 135), work each design with a separate ball of yarn, crossing the yarns where the balls meet. The yarns can be wound on to yarn bobbins to avoid tangles.

TEXTURAL EFFECTS

Try mixing different yarns to create an interesting texture. This can be in the form of stripes, separate motifs, highlights on picture sweaters, outlining shapes, or by working the collar and cuffs in a contrast yarn.

STITCH PATTERNS

You may decide to work your garment entirely in one stitch pattern. The chapter on stitch patterns offers a selection of ribs, lacy patterns and cables for you to follow. At the beginning of each set of instructions is a list of suitable garment widths and the number of selvedge stitches you will have to include when planning your design. However, as the armhole and neck shapings are worked you will have to adjust the number of selvedge stitches to fit the shape of the grid pattern. An example is the V-neck sweater front in 'mosaic tile stitch' (multiple of 4 + 2 sts).

Where the pattern shows a multiple of a number + another number, e.g. 4 + 2, the additional number of stitches (2) must be divided and placed at each end of the row when planning the layout. Then, after working the selvedge sts (usually in stocking stitch), the stitch pattern is followed.
In the V-necked sweater just mentioned, the mosaic tile stitch is followed without alteration until the 49th row. The pattern then reads:
49th row: Cast off 4 sts, k3, pattern 58, k8.
50th row: Cast off 4 sts, p3, pattern 58, p4.
51st row: Cast off 2 sts, k1, pattern 58, k4.
52nd row: Cast off 2 sts, p1, pattern 58, p2
and so on.

If you prefer to use a number of stitch patterns in one garment, outline your design on the grid pattern. If the stitch patterns you choose do not exactly match the number of stitches in the grid, use stocking stitch to fill the gaps.

SYMBOLS TO SHOW PATTERN STITCHES

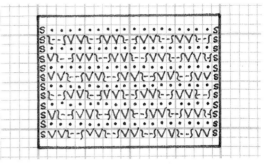

As with colour knitting, symbols can be used to denote pattern stitches.

	cross 2R
	cross 2L
	cable over 6 sts
	dec or k2 tog
	inc 1 or make 1
	inc 5
	knit
	purl
	psso
	sl 1, k1, psso
	sl 1 knitwise
	sl 1 purlwise
	k1 tbl
	turn
	y fwd
	y back
	yrn
	selvedge stitch
	st st
	rev st st

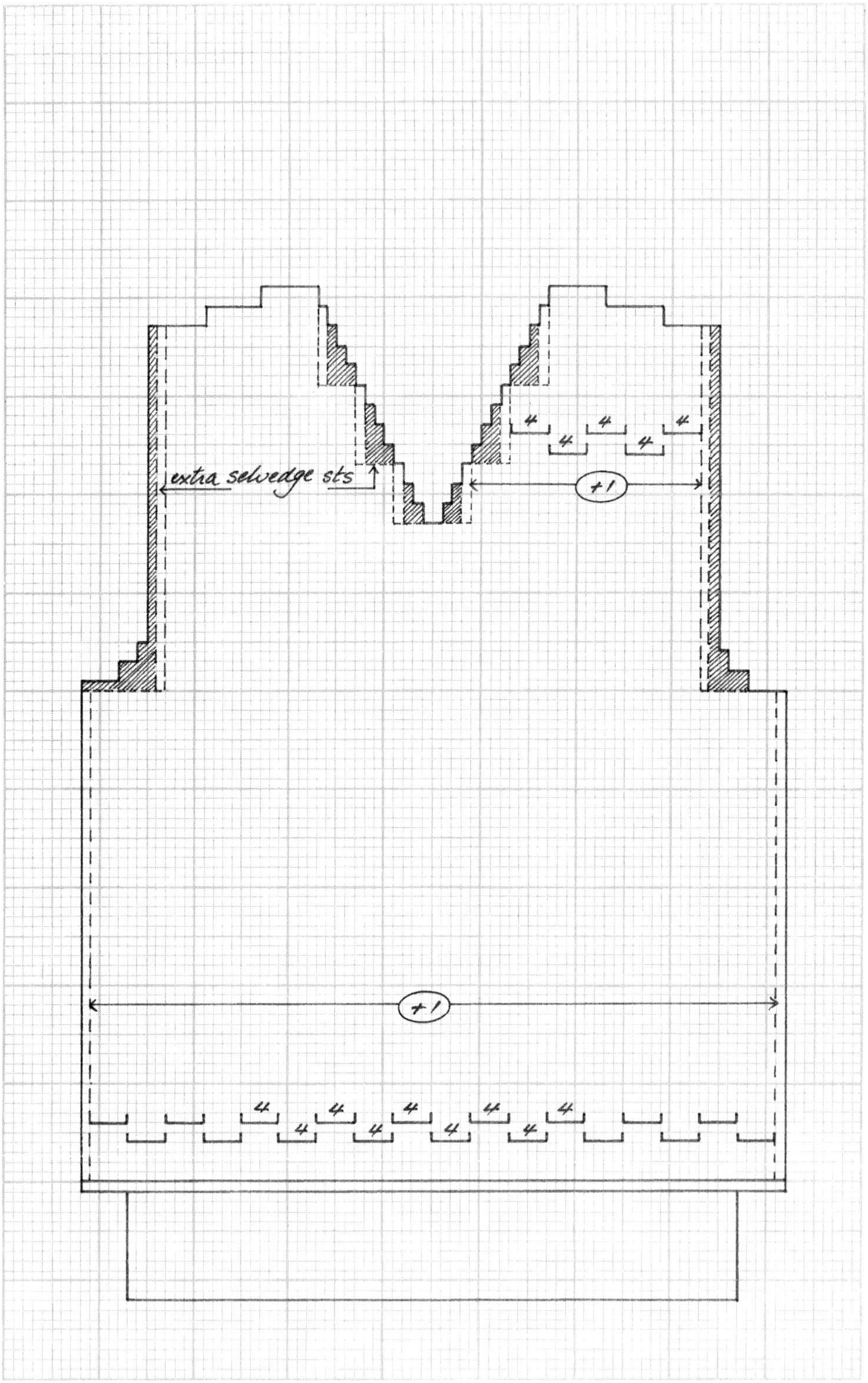

extra selvedge sts

+1

+1

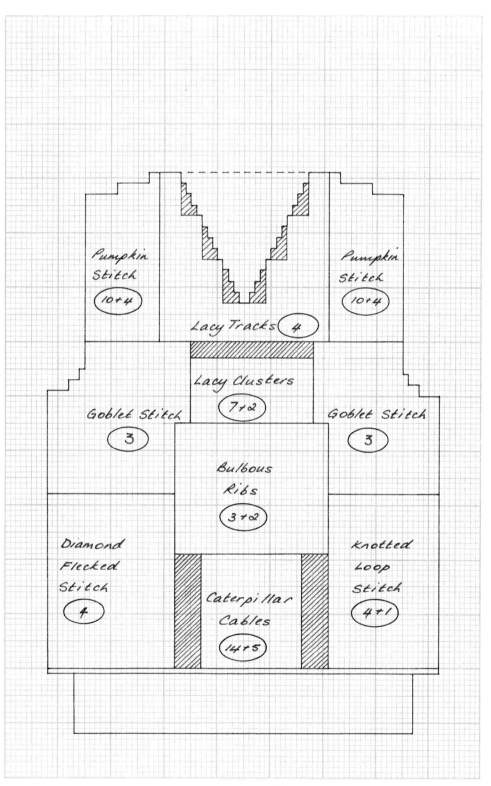

Pumpkin Stitch (10+4)

Pumpkin Stitch (10+4)

Lacy Tracks (4)

Lacy Clusters (7+2)

Goblet Stitch (3)

Goblet Stitch (3)

Bulbous Ribs (3+2)

Diamond Flecked Stitch (4)

Knotted Loop Stitch (4+1)

Caterpillar Cables (14+5)

Remember to plan your pattern from right to left when working on the right side of the garment, and from left to right on the wrong side.

This technique is particularly useful when you want to put small amounts of stitch pattern in isolated places.

HANDY TIP

Avoid using pastel colours or white as the background for a large multi-coloured garment. Unless all the colours are pastels, the stronger ones will have a tendency to show through.

7

A Directory Of Scandinavian
And Fair Isle Designs

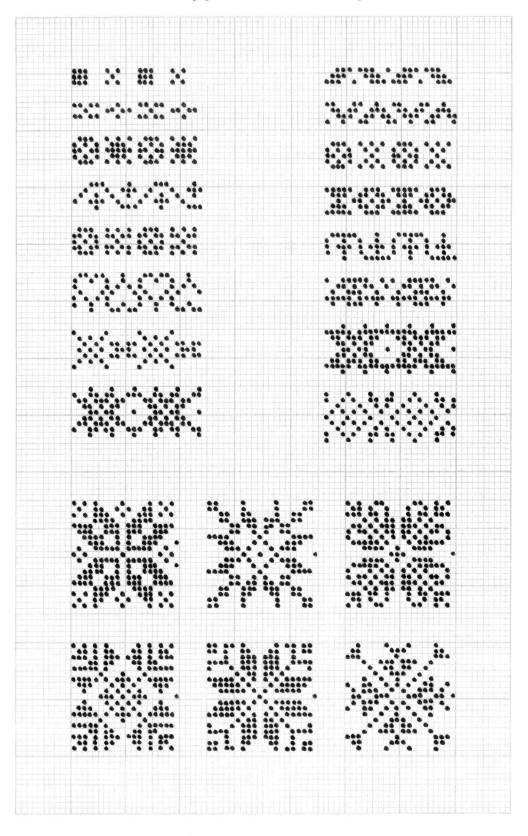

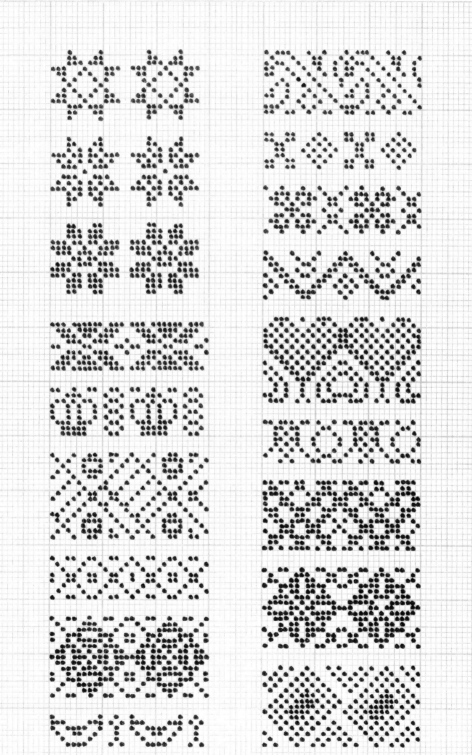

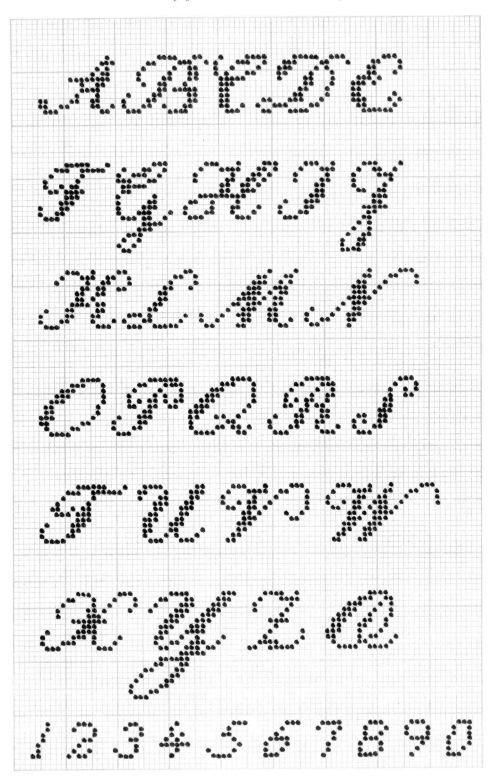

8

A DIRECTORY OF
STITCH PATTERNS

RIBS AND FANCY STITCHES

The first row of a pattern begins on the row after the casting-on row. All odd-numbered rows are on the right side of the work (unless otherwise stated); even-numbered rows are on the wrong side of the work.

Where the pattern has 'selvedge sts', divide them between the two sides of the knitting (e.g. with 76 sts including 6 selvedge sts, the row should appear as: 3 selv sts, 70 sts, 3 selv sts.

K the selvedge sts on the right side and p them on the wrong side.

** Instructions written between asterisks should be repeated as far as possible to the end of the row.

Cross 2R (on the right side of the work):
On a knit row, knit the second stitch on the left needle by passing in front of the first stitch and inserting the needle from left to right through the front loop of the stitch. Knit the first stitch and slip both stitches off the needle.

On a purl row, purl the second stitch by passing in front of the first stitch and inserting the needle from right to left through the front loop of the stitch. Purl the first stitch and slip both stitches off the needle.

Cross 2L (on the right side of the work):
On a knit row, keeping the right needle at the back of the work, pick up the front loop of the second stitch and knit it. Knit the first stitch and slip both stitches off the needle.

On a purl row, working from left to right, insert the right needle through the second and then the first stitch on the left needle. Turn the needle and then slip the stitches on to the right needle (they

are now twisted). Slip them back on to the left needle and purl them in the usual way.

1 × 1 RIB

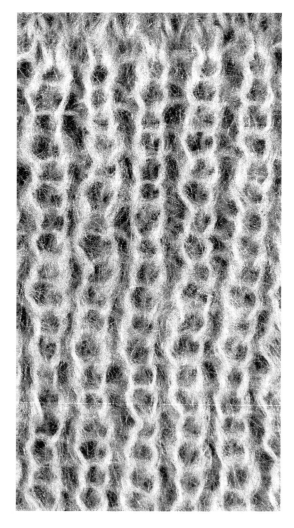

Multiple of 2:
58 sts
64 sts
66 sts
74 sts
76 sts
80 sts
160 sts

1st row: *K1, p1*.
2nd row: *P1, k1*.

1 × 1 TWISTED RIB

Multiple of 2:
58 sts
64 sts
66 sts
74 sts
76 sts
80 sts
160 sts

Work as 1 × 1 rib, working into the back of every k st.

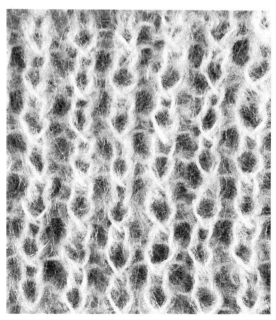

MOCK RIB

Multiple of 2:
58 sts
64 sts
66 sts
74 sts
76 sts
80 sts
160 sts

1st and alt odd rows: *P1, y bk, sl 1 purlwise, y fwd*.
2nd and alt even rows: P.

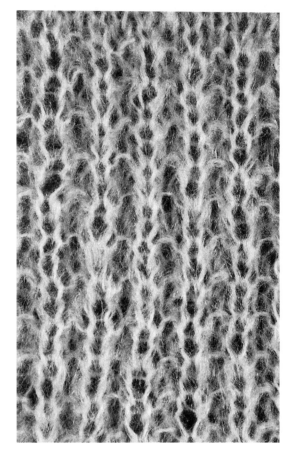

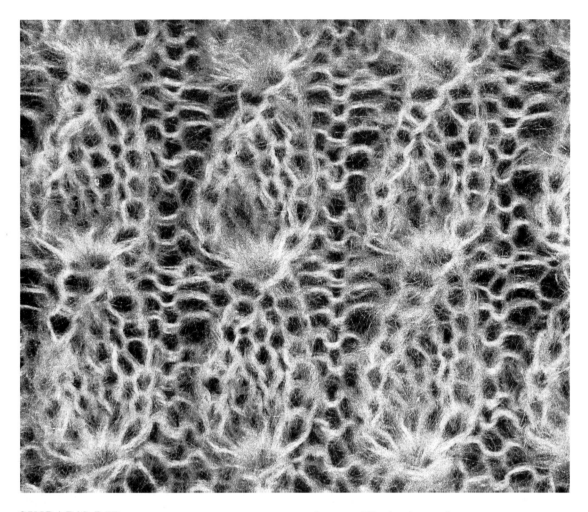

SINBAD'S RIB

Multiple of 2:
58 sts
64 sts
66 sts
74 sts
76 sts
80 sts
160 sts

1st row: *P2, k2*.
2nd and alt rows: K the p sts and p the k sts of the previous row.
3rd row: *P2, take the next 2 sts tog and work 5 sts in these 2 sts (k1, p1, k1, p1, k1)*. On following even-numbered rows p the extra sts.
5th row: *P2, k3, k2 tog*.

7th row: *P2, k2, k2 tog*.
9th row: *P2, k1, k2 tog*.
11th row: Rep from 3rd row.

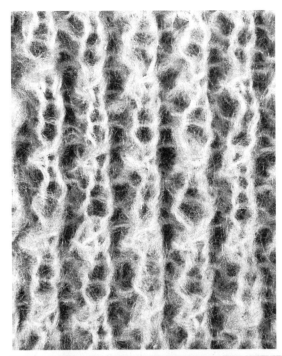

FRENCH KNOT RIB

Multiple of 2:
58 sts
64 sts
66 sts
74 sts
76 sts
80 sts
160 sts

1st and 2nd rows: *K1, p1*.
3rd row: *Work into front and back of k st, p1*.
4th row: *K1, p2 tog*.

BULBOUS RIB

Multiple of 3 + 2:
58 sts including 2 selvedge sts on the front opening side
64 sts including 2 selvedge sts
65 sts
76 sts including 2 selvedge sts
74 sts

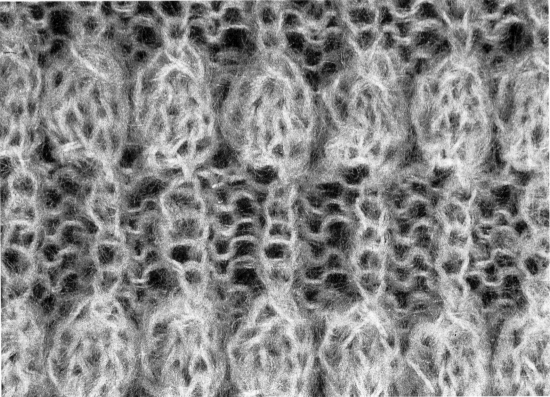

80 sts

160 sts including 2 selvedge sts

1st, 3rd and 5th rows: *P2, k1*, p2.
2nd, 4th and 6th rows: K2, *p1, k2*.
7th row: *P2, k 3 times in next st (k1 tbl, k1, k1 tbl)*, p2.
8th, 9th and 10th rows: K the p sts and p the k sts of the previous row.
11th row: *P2, sl 1, k2 tog, psso*, p2.
12th row: Rep from row 2.

3 × 1 SLIP STITCH RIB

Multiple of 4:
58 sts including 2 selvedge sts on the front opening side
66 sts including 2 selvedge sts
64 sts
74 sts including 2 selvedge sts
76 sts

80 sts

160 sts

1st row: *K3, sl 1 purlwise*.
2nd row: P.
3rd row: As 1st row.
4th row: As 2nd row.

2 × 2 RIB

Multiple of 4:
58 sts including 2 selvedge sts on the front opening side
66 sts including 2 selvedge sts
64 sts
74 sts including 2 selvedge sts
76 sts
80 sts
160 sts

1st row: *K2, p2*.
2nd row: *P2, k2*.

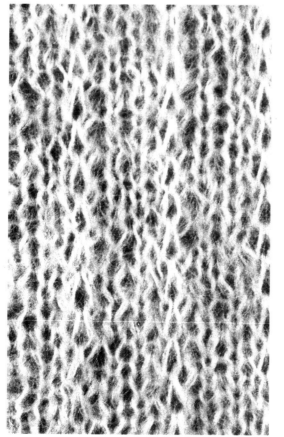

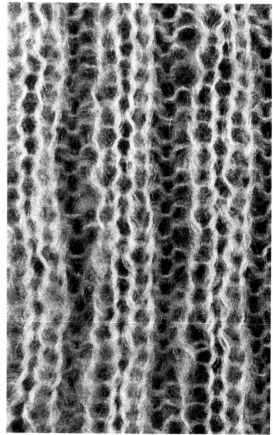

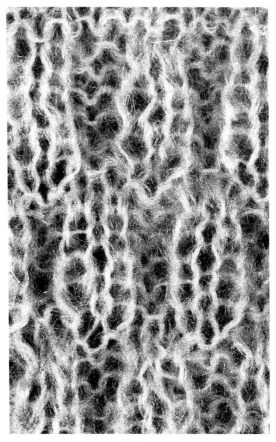
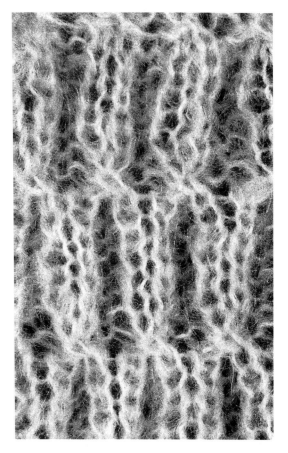

BROKEN 2 × 2 RIB

Multiple of 4:
58 sts including 2 selvedge sts on the front opening side
66 sts including 2 selvedge sts
64 sts
74 sts including 2 selvedge sts
76 sts
80 sts
160 sts

1st, 2nd, 3rd, 4th, 5th and 6th rows: *K2, p2*.
7th, 8th, 9th, 10th, 11th and 12th rows: *P2, k2*.

ALTERNATING RIB

Multiple of 4 + 2:
58 sts
64 sts including 2 selvedge sts
66 sts

74 sts
76 sts including 2 selvedge sts
80 sts including 2 selvedge sts
160 sts including 2 selvedge sts

1st, 3rd and 5th rows: *K2, p2*, k2.
2nd, 4th and 6th rows: *P2, k2*, p2.
7th row: K1, *sl the next st on to a spare needle and leave at front of work, p1, k the 2nd st on the left-hand needle and sl off over the first st, k the st from the spare needle, p1*, k1.
8th to 13th rows *inclusive*: Rep 1st to 6th rows.
14th row: *K2, p2*, k2.
15th row: K1, k the 2nd st on the left-hand needle and sl off over the first st, p1, *sl the next st on to a spare needle and leave at front of work, p1, k the 2nd st on the left-hand needle and sl off over the first st, k the st from the spare needle, p1*, sl the next st on to a spare needle and leave at front of work, p1, k the st from the spare needle, k1.
16th row: *P2, k2*, p2.

107

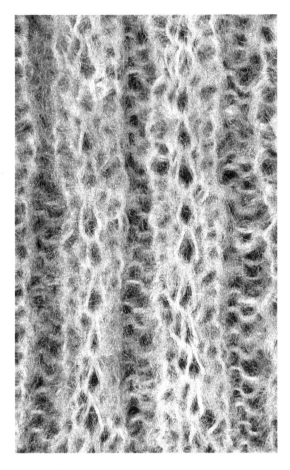
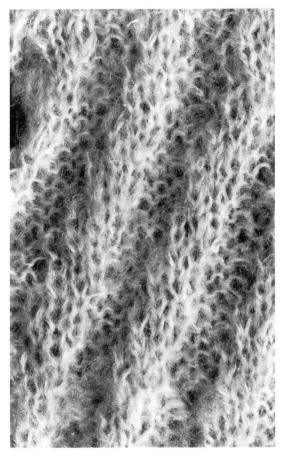

SLIP STITCH RIB

Multiple of 5:
58 sts including 3 selvedge sts on the front opening side
64 sts including 4 selvedge sts
65 sts
74 sts including 4 selvedge sts
75 sts
80 sts
160 sts

1st row: *P2, k1, sl 1, k1*
2nd row: *P3, k2*.

PISA'S RIB

Multiple of 6:
58 sts including 4 selvedge sts on the front opening side
64 sts including 4 selvedge sts
66 sts
74 sts including 2 selvedge sts
76 sts including 4 selvedge sts
80 sts including 2 selvedge sts
160 sts including 4 selvedge sts

1st, 2nd and 3rd rows: *K3, p3*.
4th and 6th rows: *P1, k3, p2*.
5th, 8th, 14th and 17th rows: K the p sts and p the k sts of the previous row.
7th and 9th rows: *K1, p3, k2*.
10th, 11th and 12th rows: *P3, k3*.
13th and 15th rows: *P2, k3, p1*.
16th and 18th rows: *K2, p3, k1*.
19th row: Rep from 1st row.

6. 'Czech'

7. 'Scandi' (right) and 'Flight'

8. 'Viking'

9. 'Snowflake'

SPIRAL RIB

Multiple of 7:
58 sts including 2 selvedge sts on the front opening side
65 sts including 2 selvedge sts
74 sts including 4 selvedge sts
76 sts including 6 selvedge sts
160 sts including 6 selvedge sts

1st row: *Cross 2L, k3, p2*
2nd and alt rows: *K2, p5*.
3rd row: *K1, cross 2L, k2, p2*.
5th row: *K2, cross 2L, k1, p2*.
7th row: *K3, cross 2L, p2*.
9th row: Rep from 1st row.

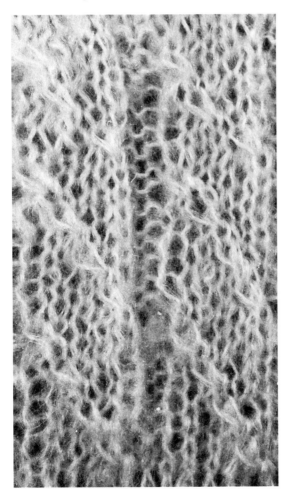

GARTER LACE STITCH

Multiple of 2:
58 sts
74 sts
76 sts
80 sts
160 sts

1st row: K1, *k3, k2 tog, yrn to make 1 st, k1*.
2nd and 5th rows: P.
3rd and 6th rows: K.
4th row: *K4, k2 tog, m 1*, k1.

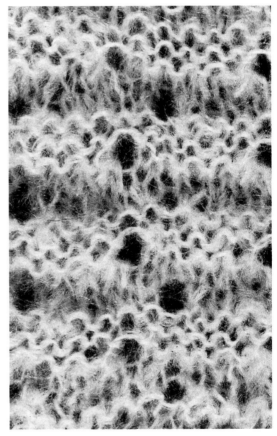

BAMBOO STITCH

Multiple of 2:
58 sts
64 sts
66 sts
74 sts
76 sts
80 sts
160 sts

1st row: *Yrn to make one, k2, pass made st over k2*.
2nd and alt rows: P.

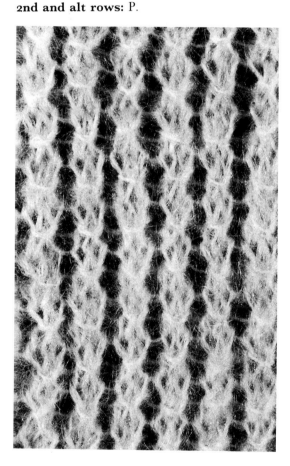

GOBLET STITCH

Multiple of 3:
58 sts including one selvedge st on the seam side
74 sts including 2 selvedge sts
75 sts
76 sts including 4 selvedge sts
80 sts including 2 selvedge sts
160 sts including 4 selvedge sts

1st row (wrong side): K.
2nd row: *K3 tog and leave st on left-hand needle, k the first of 3 sts, k next 2 tog tbl*.
3rd row: P.
4th row: K.

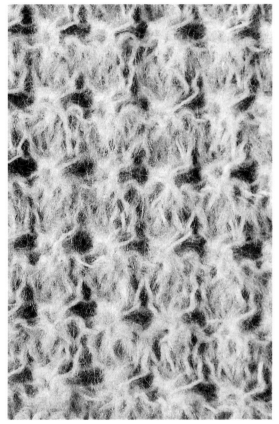

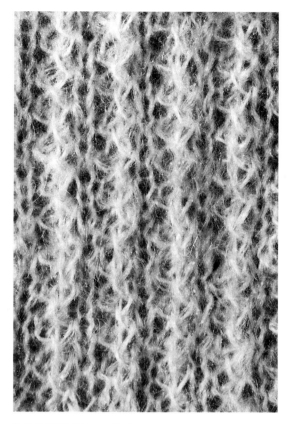

RABBITS' EAR STITCH

Multiple of 3 + 1:
58 sts
66 sts including 2 selvedge sts
64 sts
75 sts including 2 selvedge sts
76 sts

1st row: *K1, sl 1 purlwise, k1, pass sl st over k1,
put it on to left-hand needle and k it*.
2nd row: P.

TEAR DROPS

Multiple of 3 + 1:
58 sts
75 sts including 2 selvedge sts
80 sts including 4 selvedge sts
160 sts

1st, 5th and 9th rows: K.
2nd, 6th and 10th rows: P.
3rd row: K1, *insert right-hand needle between

the 2nd and 3rd sts and draw through a loop,
leaving loop on right-hand needle, k3*.
4th row: P1, *p2, p2 tog*.
7th row: K2, *insert right-hand needle between
the 2nd and 3rd sts and draw through a loop as
before, k3*, k2.
8th row: *P2, p2 tog*.
11th row: *Insert right-hand needle between the
2nd and 3rd sts and draw through a loop, k3*, k1.
12th row: P2, *p2, p2 tog*, k the last loop with
the first selvedge st.

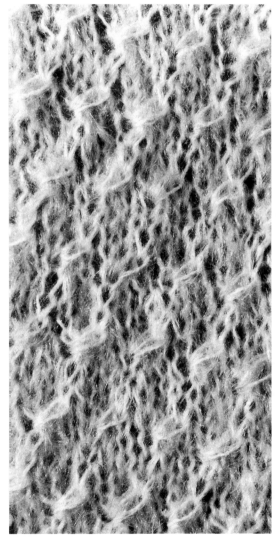

SPIRAL STAIRCASE (*1*)

Multiple of 4:
58 sts including 2 selvedge sts
76 sts
74 sts including 2 selvedge sts
80 sts
160 sts

1st row: K.
2nd row: *P4, yrn to m 1*.
3rd row: *Drop the made st of the previous row, yrn to m 1, sl 1, k3, psso*.
4th row: P.

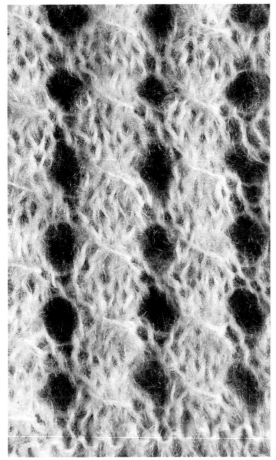

DIAMOND FLECKED STITCH

Multiple of 4:
58 sts including 2 selvedge sts
74 sts including 2 selvedge sts
76 sts
80 sts
160 sts

1st and alt rows: K.
2nd row: *Yrn to make one, p2, pass made st over p2, p2*.
4th row: *P2, m 1, p2, pass made st over p2*.

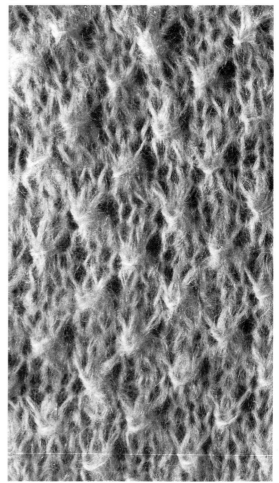

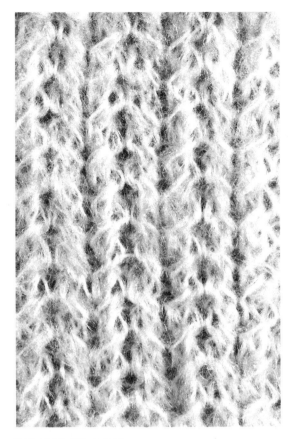

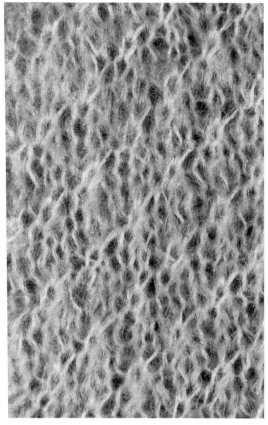

LEAFY PLAITS

Multiple of 4:
58 sts including 2 selvedge sts
74 sts including 2 selvedge sts
76 sts
80 sts
160 sts

1st row: *Cross 2R, cross 2L*.
2nd row: P.

SIDE SLIP STITCH

Multiple of 4:
58 sts including 2 selvedge sts
74 sts including 2 selvedge sts
76 sts
80 sts
160 sts

1st row: *K2 tog then k the 1st of these 2 sts again, k2*.
2nd and 4th row: P.
3rd row: *K2, k2 tog then k the 1st of these 2 sts again*.

HORNET'S NEST

Multiple of 4:
58 sts including 2 selvedge sts
74 sts including 2 selvedge sts
76 sts
80 sts
160 sts

1st row: *Cross 2R, cross 2L*.
2nd and alt rows: P.
3rd row: *Cross 2L, cross 2R*.

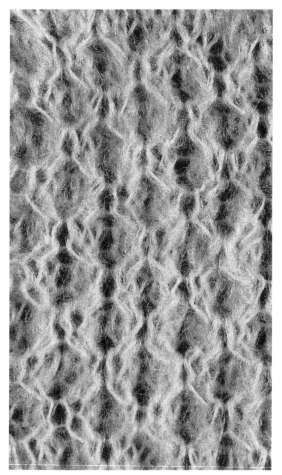

LACY TRACKS

Multiple of 4:
58 sts including 2 selvedge sts on the front opening side
66 sts including 2 selvedge sts
64 sts
74 sts including 2 selvedge sts
76 sts
80 sts
160 sts

1st and 3rd rows: *K1, p3*.
2nd, 4th and 6th rows: *K3, p1*.
5th row: *K1, p2 tog, yrn to make one, p1*.

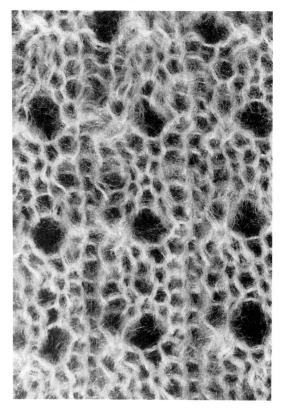

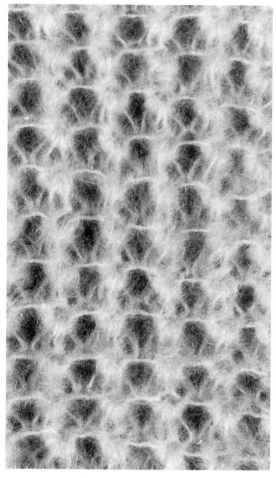

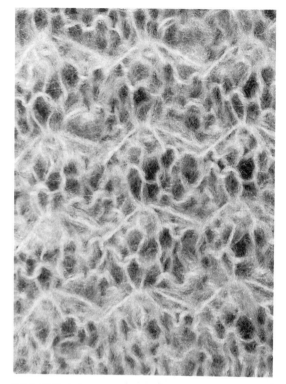

KNOTTED LOOP STITCH

Multiple of 4 + 1:
58 sts including one selvedge st on the front opening side
65 sts
75 sts including 2 selvedge sts

1st row (wrong side): K1, *p3 tog keeping the sts on the left-hand needle, k them tog and p them tog again, k1*.
2nd and alt rows: P.
13th row: *P2, k1, k tog 2 stranded loops and next st as 7th row*.
15th row: Repeat from 3rd row.

TEEPEE STITCH

Multiple of 4 + 2 selvedge sts:
58 sts
74 sts
76 sts including 4 selvedge sts
80 sts including 4 selvedge sts
160 sts including 4 selvedge sts

1st, 2nd, 5th, 6th, 8th, 11th, 12th and 14th rows: *P2, k2*.
3rd and 9th rows: *P2, y fwd, sl 2 purlwise*.
4th and 10th rows: *Y bk, sl 2, k2*.
7th row: *P2, k tog the 2 stranded loops of the previous 2 rows and the next st, k1*.
13th row: *P2, k1, k tog 2 stranded loops and next st as 7th row.
15th row: Repeat from 3rd row.

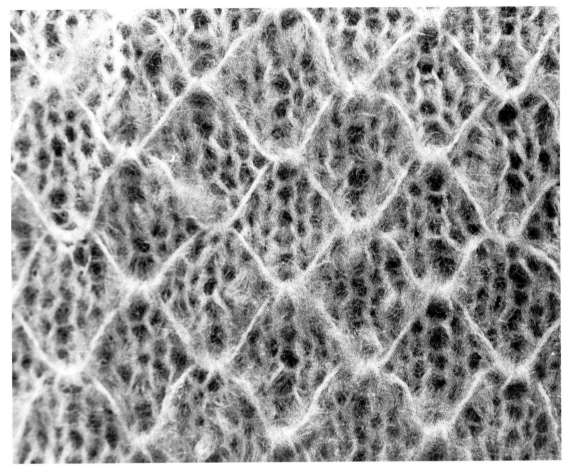

MOSAIC TILE STITCH

Multiple of 4 + 2:
58 sts
74 sts
76 sts including 2 selvedge sts
80 sts including 2 selvedge sts
160 sts including 2 selvedge sts

1st row: *K1, y fwd, sl 3 purlwise, take thread in front of 3 sl sts and wind round right-hand needle once*, k2.

2nd row: P letting the extra loop fall to back of work.

3rd row: K.

4th row: P.

5th row: K2, *with point of right-hand needle take up long thread and k with next st, y fwd, sl 3 purlwise taking thread across 3 sl sts, wind once round right-hand needle*.

6th row: As 2nd row.

7th row: K.

8th row: P.

9th row: K1, *y fwd, sl 3 purlwise taking thread across 3 sl sts, wind once round right-hand needle, with point of right-hand needle take up long thread and k with next st*, k1.

Repeat from 2nd row.

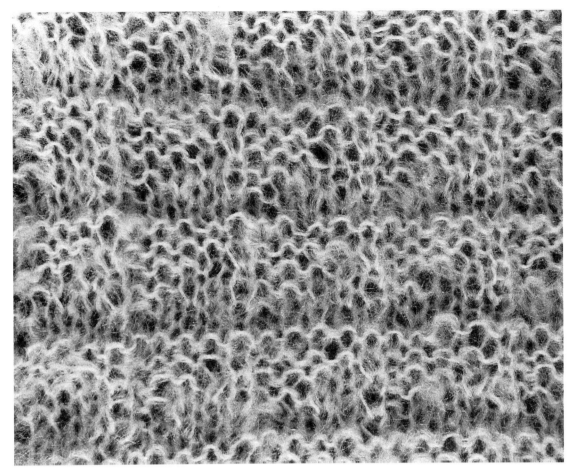

TRIANGULAR CHECK STITCH

Multiple of 5:
58 sts including 3 selvedge sts on the front opening
side
64 sts including 4 selvedge sts
65 sts
74 sts including 4 selvedge sts
75 sts
80 sts
160 sts

1st row: K.
2nd row: *K1, p4*.
3rd row: *K3, p2*.
4th row: *K3, p2*.
5th row: *K1, p4*.
6th row: K.

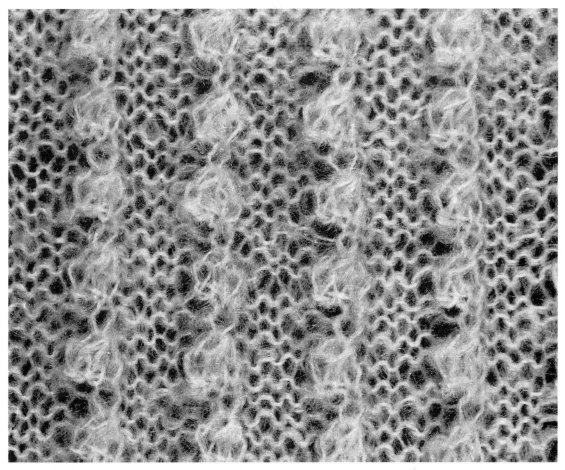

LADDERED LOZENGE STITCH

Multiple of 5:
58 sts including 3 selvedge sts on the front opening
side
64 sts including 4 selvedge sts
65 sts
74 sts including 4 selvedge sts
75 sts
80 sts
160 sts

1st row: *P4, k into front and back and front
again of next st*.
2nd row: *P3, k4*.
3rd row: *P4, k3 tog*.
4th row: *P1, k4*.

DROPLET STITCH

Multiple of 5:

58 sts including 3 selvedge sts on the seam side
74 sts including 4 selvedge sts
75 sts
76 sts including 6 selvedge sts
80 sts
160 sts

1st row: *K3, yrn to make one, k2 tog*.
2nd and alt rows: P.
3rd row: K1, *m 1, k2 tog, k3*, k4.
5th row: K4, *m 1, k2 tog, k3*, k1.
7th row: K2, *m 1, k2 tog, k3*, k3.
9th row: *M 1, k2 tog, k3*.

BASKET STITCH

Multiple of 6:

58 sts including 4 selvedge sts
74 sts including 2 selvedge sts
76 sts including 4 selvedge sts
80 sts including 2 selvedge sts
160 sts including 4 selvedge sts

1st and 7th rows: K.
2nd and 8th rows: P.
3rd and 5th rows: *K1, p4, k1*.
4th and 6th rows: *P1, k4, p1*.
9th and 11th rows: *P2, k2, p2*.
10th and 12th rows: *K2, p2, k2*.

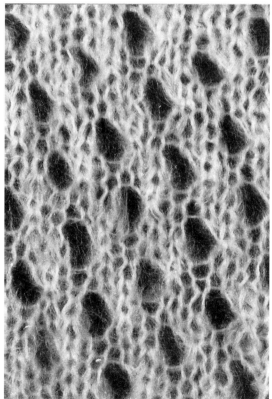

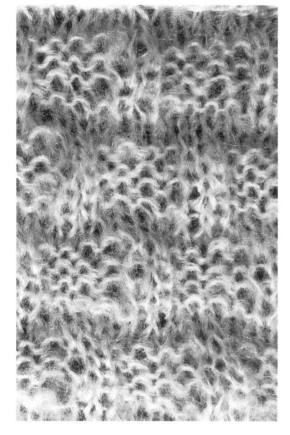

119

LAVENDER STITCH

Multiple of 6 + 1:
58 sts including 3 selvedge sts on the seam side
75 sts including 2 selvedge sts

1st, 2nd, 3rd, 4th, 5th and 12th rows: K.
6th 8th and 10th rows: P.
7th and 9th rows: *K1, y fwd, k1, sl 1, k2 tog, psso, k1, y fwd*, k1.
11th row: *K1, inc 1 (keeping inc st on left-hand needle), k1, sl 1, k2 tog, psso, k1, inc 1*, k1.

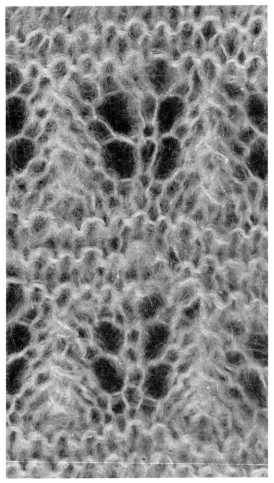

MEDALLION STITCH

Multiple of 6 + 1:
58 sts including 3 selvedge sts on the seam side
75 sts including 2 selvedge sts

1st and 3rd rows: *K1, y fwd, sl 1, k1, psso, k1, k2 tog, y fwd*, k1.
2nd and alt rows: P.
5th row: *K2, y fwd, sl 1, k2 tog, psso, y fwd, k1*, k1.
7th and 9th rows: *K1, k2 tog, y fwd, k1, y fwd, sl 1, k1, psso*, k1.
11th row: K2 tog, y fwd, *k3, y fwd, sl 1, k2 tog, psso, y fwd*, k3, y fwd, sl 1, k1, psso.

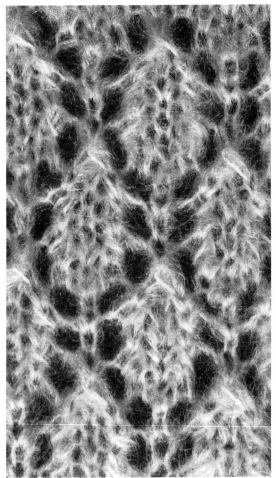

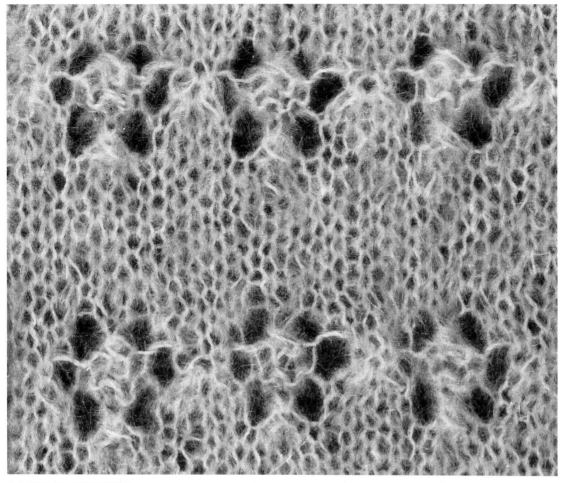

LACY CLUSTERS

Multiple of 7 + 2:
58 sts
74 sts including 2 selvedge sts
76 sts including 4 selvedge sts
160 sts including 2 selvedge sts

1st to 8th rows (inclusive): St st.
9th and 13th rows: *K2, y fwd, sl 1, k2 tog, psso, y fwd, k2*, k2.
10th and 14th rows: P.
11th row: *K2 tog, yrn, p3, y fwd, sl 1, k1, psso*, k2.
12th row: P2, *p1, k5, p1*.

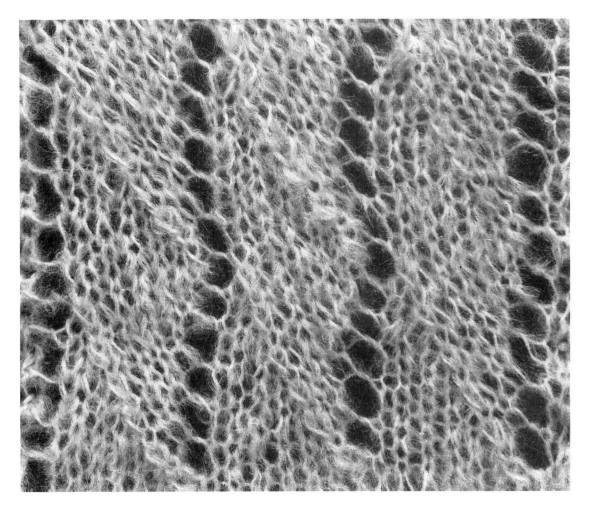

SHELL STITCH

Multiple of 7 + 4:
74 sts
76 sts including 2 selvedge sts
160 sts including 2 selvedge sts

1st row: K2, *yrn to make one, sl 1, k1, psso, k5*, m 1, k2 tog.
2nd and alt rows: P.
3rd row: K2, *m 1, k1, sl 1, k1, psso, k4*, m 1, k2 tog.
5th row: K2, *m 1, k2, sl 1, k1, psso, k3*, m 1, k2 tog.
7th row: K2, *m 1, k3, sl 1, k1, psso, k2*, m 1, k2 tog.
9th row: K2, *m 1, k4, sl 1, k1, psso, k1*, m 1, k2 tog.

11th row: K2, *m 1, k5, sl 1, k1, psso*, m 1, k2 tog.

This stitch has a tendency to slant, so should not be used for large areas.

CRYSTAL BANDS

Multiple of 8:
58 sts including 2 selvedge sts
74 sts including 2 selvedge sts
76 sts including 4 selvedge sts
80 sts
160 sts

(K 1 row and p 2 rows) twice.
1st and 9th rows: *K3, yrn to make 1 st, sl 1, k1, psso, k3*.
2nd and alt rows: P.
3rd and 7th rows: *K2, (m 1, sl 1, k1, psso) twice, k2*.
5th row: *K1 (m 1, sl 1, k1, psso) 3 times, k1*.
10th to 14 rows (inclusive): P 2 rows, k one row, p 2 rows.

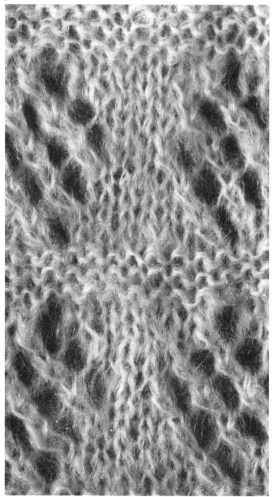

MOSSY PEAKS

Multiple of 8 + 1:
58 sts including one selvedge st on the seam side
75 sts including 2 selvedge sts

Work 8 rows in moss stitch.
1st row of pattern: *K1, yrn to make 1 st, sl 1, k1, psso, k3, k2 tog, m 1*, k1.
2nd and alt rows: P.
3rd row: *K2, m 1, sl 1, k1, psso, k1, k2 tog, m 1, k1*, k1.
5th row: *K3, m 1, sl 1, k2 tog, psso, m 1, k2*, k1.

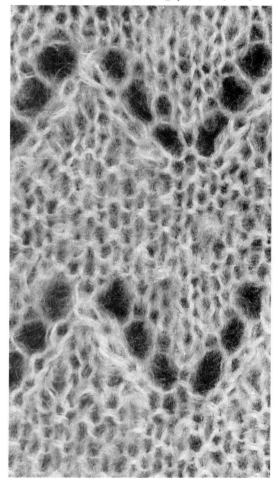

LACY LANES

Multiple of 12:
74 sts including 2 selvedge sts
76 sts including 4 selvedge sts
160 sts including 4 selvedge sts

1st row: *K3, yrn to make 1 st, sl 1, k1, psso, k2, k2 tog, m 1, k1, m 1, sl 1, k1, psso*.
2nd and alt rows: P.
3rd row: *K1, k2 tog, m 1, k1, m 1, sl 1, k1, psso, k1, k2 tog, m 1, k1, m 1, sl 1, k1, psso*.
5th row: K2 tog, m 1, k3, m 1, sl 1, k1, psso, k2 tog, m 1, k1, m 1, sl 1, k1, psso*.

BOBBLES

Pattern up to the point where you would like the bobble to be.
Inc five times into the next stitch, turn (6 sts).
P6, turn.
K6, turn.
P6, turn.
K6 tog and continue to pattern.

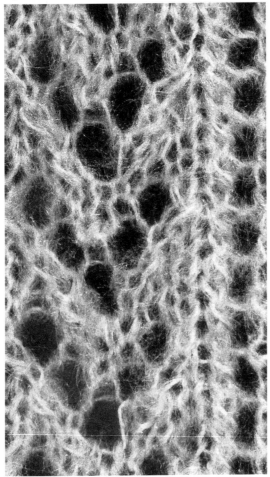

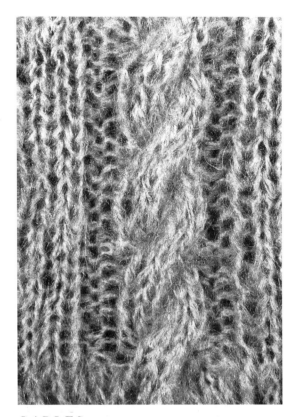

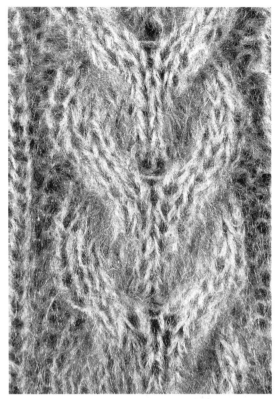

CABLES

SIMPLE CABLE

Worked over a panel of 8 sts plus 2. The crossing can be irregularly spaced.

1st row (right side): P2, *k6, p2*.
2nd row: K2, *p6, k2*.
3rd row (crossing row): P2, *sl next 3 sts on to a cable needle and leave at back of work, k3, k3 from cable needle, p2*.
4th row: As 2nd row.
Repeat 1st and 2nd rows until you want to make another crossing, then repeat 3rd and 4th rows.

For forward crossing leave stitches on the cable needle at the front of the work in the crossing row.

DOUBLE CABLE

Worked over a panel of 14 sts plus 2.

1st row: P2, *k12, p2*.
2nd row: K2, *p12, k2*.
3rd row: P2, *sl next 3 sts on to a cable needle and leave at back of work, k3, k3 from cable needle, sl next 3 sts on to a cable needle and leave at front of work, k3, k3 from cable needle, p2*.
4th row: As 2nd row.
Repeat 1st and 2nd rows until you want to make another crossing, then repeat 3rd and 4th rows.

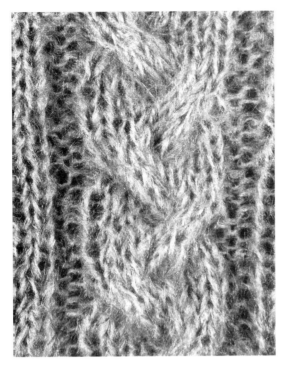

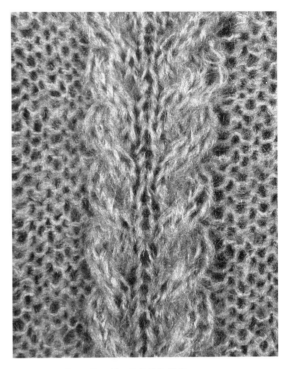

PLAITED CABLE

Worked over a panel of 11 sts plus 2.

1st row: P2, *k9, p2*.
2nd row: K2, *p9, k2*.
3rd row: P2, *sl next 3 sts on to a cable needle and leave at back of work, k3, k3 from cable needle, k3, p2*.
4th row: As 2nd row.
5th row: As 1st row.
6th row: As 2nd row.
7th row: P2, *k3, sl next 3 sts on to a cable needle and leave at front of work, k3, k3 from cable needle, p2*.
8th row: As 2nd row.

CATERPILLAR CABLES

Worked over a panel of 14 + 5.

1st row: *P5, k9*, p5.
2nd and alt rows: K the p sts and p the k sts of the previous row.
3rd row: *P5, sl 2 sts on to a cable needle and leave at front of work, k next 2 sts, k2 from cable needle, k1, sl 2 sts on to a cable needle and leave at back of work, k next 2 sts, k2 from cable needle*, p5.

MONOCLES

Worked over a panel of 18 sts.

1st row: P3, k3, (k1, p1) 3 times, k3, p3.
2nd row: K3, p3, (k1, p1) 3 times, p3, k3.
3rd row: As 1st row.
4th row: As 2nd row.
5th row: P3, sl 3 sts on to cable needle and leave at back of work, work next 3 sts in moss st, k3 from cable needle, sl 3 sts on to cable needle and leave at front of work, k next 3 sts, work in moss st the 3 sts from cable needle, p3.
6th, 8th, 10th, 12th and 14th rows: K3, work 3 sts in moss st, p6, 3 sts in moss st, k3.
7th, 9th, 11th and 13th rows: P3, work 3 sts in moss st, k6, 3 sts in moss st, p3.
15th row: P3, sl 3 sts on to cable needle and leave at front of work, k next 3 sts, work in moss st the 3 sts from the cable needle, sl 3 sts on to cable needle and leave at back of work, work next 3 sts in moss st, k3 sts from cable needle, p3.
16th, 18th, 20th, 22nd, 24th, 26th and 28th rows: K3, p3, (k1, p1) 3 times, p3, k3.
17th, 19th, 21st, 23rd, 25th and 27th rows: P3, k3, (k1, p1) 3 times, k3, p3.
29th row: Repeat from 5th row.

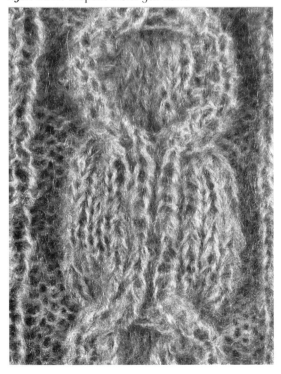

PUMPKIN STITCH

Multiple of 10 + 4:
58 sts including 4 selvedge sts (on the seam side)
74 sts
76 sts including 2 selvedge sts
80 sts including 6 selvedge sts
160 sts including 6 selvedge sts

1st row (wrong side of work): P4, *k6, p4*.
2nd row: *Yrn to make 1 st, k2 tog tbl, k2 tog, yrn to m 1, p2, (k1, p1, k1 into next st) twice, p2*, m 1, k2 tog tbl, k2 tog, m 1.
3rd row: P4, *k2, p6, k2, p4*.
4th row: *Yrn to m 1, k2 tog tbl, k2 tog, m 1, p2, k6, p2*, yrn to m 1, k2 tog tbl, k2 tog, m 1.
5th row: As 3rd row.
6th row: As 4th row.
7th row: As 3rd row.
8th row: *Yrn to m 1, k2 tog tbl, k2 tog, m 1, p2, (k3 tog) twice, p2*, yrn to m 1, k2 tog tbl, k2 tog, m 1.
9th row: As 1st row.
10th row: Yrn to m 1, k2 tog tbl, k2 tog, m 1, p6*, yrn to m 1, k2 tog tbl, k2 tog, m 1.

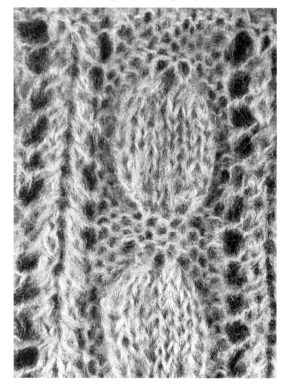

MEDUSA'S CABLE

Multiple of 12:
58 sts – add 2 extra sts to the front edge to make 60 sts
74 sts including 2 selvedge sts
76 sts including 4 selvedge sts
80 sts including 8 selvedge sts
160 sts including 4 selvedge sts

1st row: K.
2nd and alt rows: P.
3rd row: *Sl next 3 sts on to a cable needle and leave at front of work, k3, k3 from cable needle, k6*.
5th row: K.
7th row: *K6, sl next 3 sts on to a cable needle and leave at back of work, k3, k3 from cable needle.
8th row: P.

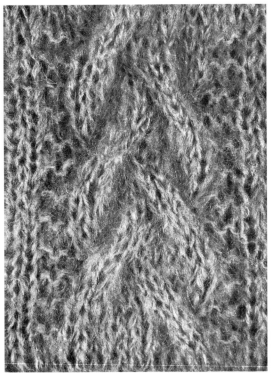

TWO-COLOUR CABLE

Multiple of 12 + 2:
58 sts including 8 selvedge sts on the seam side
74 sts
76 sts including 2 selvedge sts
80 sts including 6 selvedge sts
160 sts including 6 selvedge sts

M = main colour
C = second colour

1st row: *K2M, p2M, k2C, k2M, k2C, p2M*, k2M.
2nd and alt rows: K the p sts and p the k sts of the previous row using the same colours.
3rd row: As 1st row.
5th row: *K2M, p2M, sl 4 sts on to cable needle and leave at front of work, k next 2C sts, sl the 2M sts from cable needle to left needle and knit them with M, k2C sts from cable needle, p2M*, k2M.
7th row: As 2nd row.
9th row: Repeat from 1st row.

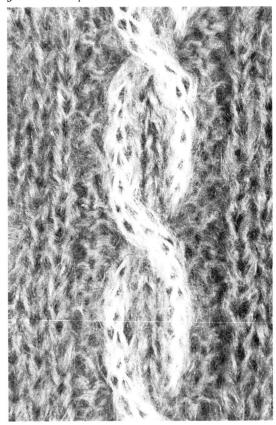

128

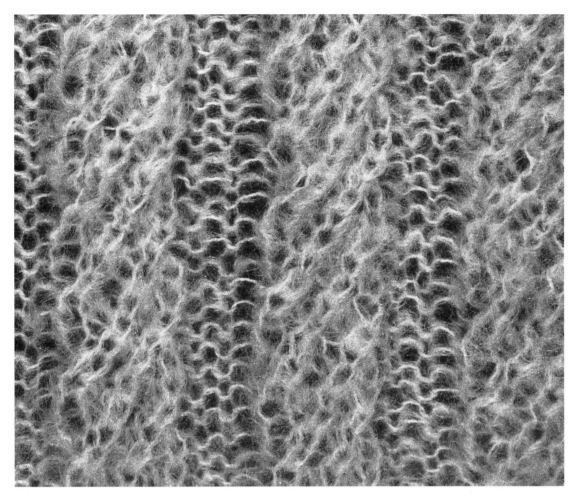

SPIRAL STAIRCASE *(2)*

Multiple of 8 + 3:
75 sts

1st row: *P3, k5*, p3.
2nd and alt rows: *K3, p5*, k3.
3rd row: *P3, k1, (k into second st then k into first st) twice*, p3.
5th row: *P3, (k into second st then k into first st) twice, k1*, p3.
7th row: Repeat from 3rd row.

· 9 ·
EXAMPLES OF THE TECHNIQUE

THE SWEATERS

'PEACH'

See photograph opposite. (Example fits 97–102 cm/38–40 in. chest).

390 g (780 m) Jonelle Mohair
50 g random colour yarn

- **V-neck pattern** divided down centre front to form a cardigan
- full sleeves in concertina rib (see Concertina collar)
- single rib cuffs
- shawl collar (ridged), including front bands
- picot-edged hem with random colour yarn ribbed belt inserted and tying at front
- random colour yarn triangles scattered over the garment at the end

'JADE'

See colour plate 1 (Example fits 97–102 cm/38–40 in. chest.)

900 g (1350 m) Pingouin 'Contrastes'
1 button
40 cm × 2 cm-wide elastic

- **one-piece jacket**
- pattern extended to coat length
- full sleeves
- picot-edged cuffs with 2 cm-wide elastic inserted
- simple ribbed band collar
- horizontal button bands
- patch pockets

'LESOTHO BLUE'

See colour plate 4. (Example fits 102–107 cm/40–42 in. chest.)

1000 g (800 m) Lesotho Handspun 'le Mohair'

- **raglan body pattern**
- raglan sleeves
- 2 × 2 rib cuffs and welt
- 'afterthought' pocket
- neck and pocket edged in suede

'SIBERIA'

See colour plate 2. (Example fits 107–112 cm/42–44 in. chest.)

470 g (1034 m) Patons 'Siberia'

- **raglan pattern**
- raglan sleeves
- 2 × 2 rib cuffs and welt
- horizontal cable collar
- cabling along the decreasing edges of front and sleeves

'WHISPER'

See colour plate 5. (Example fits 87–92 cm/34–36 in. chest.)

360 g (756 m) Jaeger 'Mohair Gold'

- **dolman pattern**
- single rib cuffs grafted on to sleeves
- loopy collar
- single rib welt

' (*Photograph by Robin Thompson*)

'FEATHERS' (*Photograph by Robin Thompson*)

(Example fits 87–92 cm/34–36 in. chest.)

500 g (900 m) British Mohair Spinners Mohair
25 g Feather yarn

- **dolman pattern** extended to dress length
- single rib cuffs grafted on to sleeve
- swollen rib collar
- feather yarn worked across alternate stitches along centre sleeve row

10. 'Eagle'

11. 'Triangles'

12. 'Moonlight'

13. 'Stained glass'

14. 'Soraya' (left) and 'Midnight'

'CZECH'

See colour plate 6. (Example fits 92–97 cm/36–38 in. chest.)

450 g (900 m) Jonelle Mohair
25 g cotton yarn

KEY:
background = white

□	●	✖	·	○
red	blue	green	yellow	black chain stitch

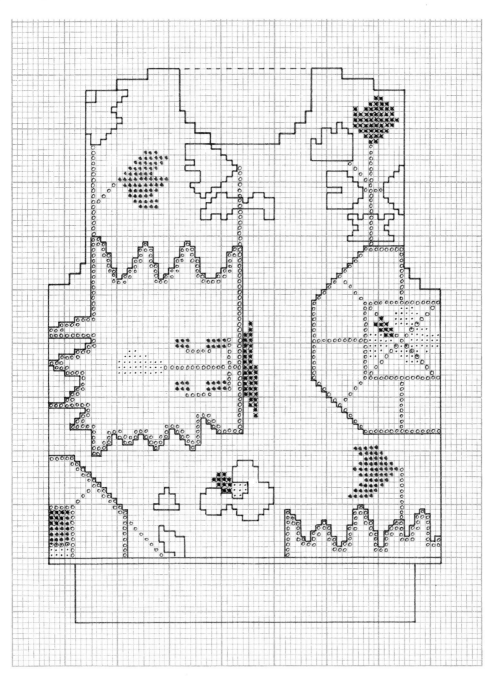

250 g (500 m) white
125 g (250 m) red
 25 g (50 m) bright blue
 25 g (50 m) green
 25 g (50 m) black
 25 g (50 m) bright yellow cotton yarn

- **round neck pattern**
- blouse sleeves
- single rib cuffs and welt
- side slit collar
- embroidered chain stitch to outline motifs
- small balls of yarn used for isolated motifs
- combination of blocked pattern and symbols
- back and front alike, but begin stocking stitch on back with a purl row and omit the neck shaping

KEY:
background = white

□	●	✖	·	○
red	blue	green	yellow	black chain stitch

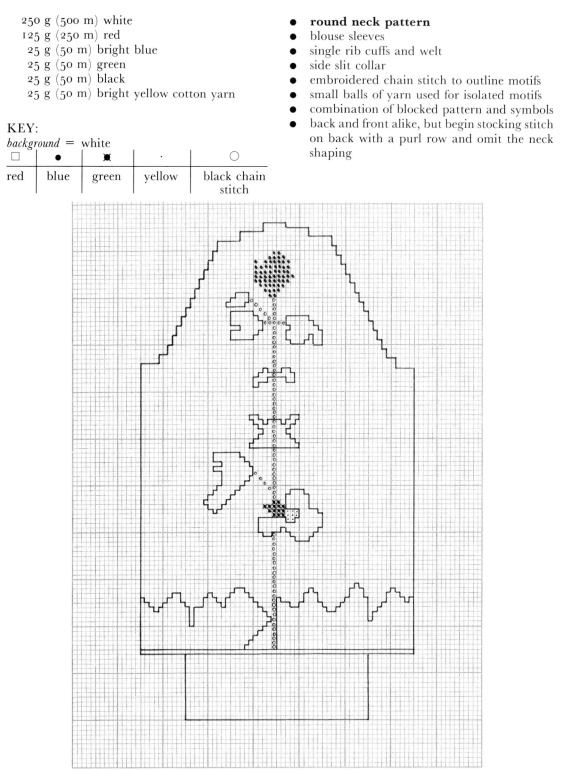

'FLIGHT'

See colour plate 7. (Example fits 112–117 cm/44–46 in. chest *or*, reduced with epaulettes, 92–97 cm/36–38 in. chest as a coat.)

700 g (1400 m) Jonelle Mohair
550 g (1100 m) navy
50 g (110 m) cerise
50 g (110 m) light brown
50 g (110 m) bright blue
14 buttons

KEY:
background = navy

×	·	∪
cerise	light brown	bright blue

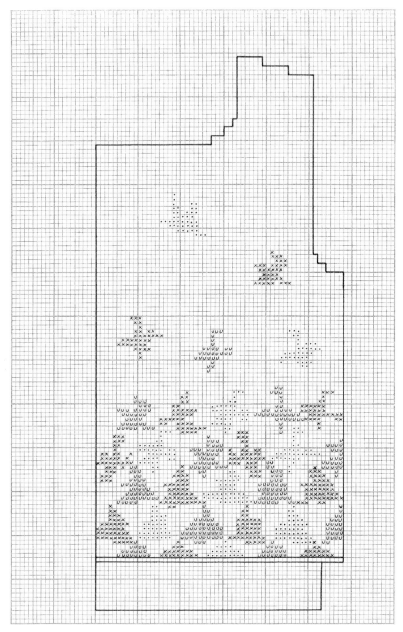

- **crossover jacket pattern**
- shirt sleeve
- single rib cuffs and welt
- shawl collar (stocking stitch)
- plain vertical button bands
- epaulettes used to draw in the shoulders to create a coat
- small balls of yarn for each motif

KEY:

background = navy

×	.	∪
cerise	light brown	bright blue

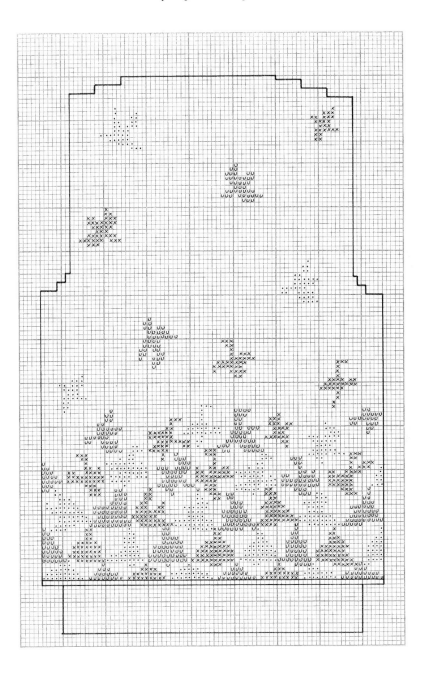

137

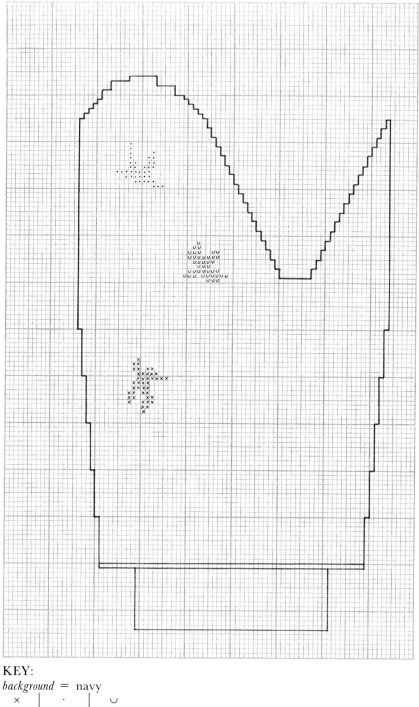

KEY:

background = navy

×	·	∪
cerise	light brown	bright blue

'SCANDI'

See colour plate 7. (Example fits 77–82 cm/30–32 in. chest.)

600 g (1200 m) Jonelle Mohair
  425 g (850 m) white

75 g (150 m) red
50 g (100 m) bright blue
50 g (100 m) mink
10 g bright yellow linen yarn
14 buttons

KEY:

background = white

×	●	○	·
red	blue	mink	yellow

- **crossover jacket pattern**
- for right front begin first row of stocking stitch
  after the increase row as: P

- shirt sleeve with seam outlined in embroidered chain stitch and buttoned cuff
- single rib cuffs and welt
- shawl collar (stocking stitch)
- plain vertical button bands

KEY:
background = white

×	●	○	.
red	blue	mink	yellow

'TRIANGLES'

See colour plate 11. (Example fits 92–97 cm/36–38 in. chest).

510 g (918 m) British Mohair Spinners Mohair
   150 g (270 m) toffee
   140 g (252 m) light grey
   110 g (198 m) dark grey
   110 g (198 m) cream

- **V-neck pattern**
- shaped sleeve
- single rib cuffs and welt
- overlapping V collar

KEY:

□	•	·	+
toffee	light grey	dark grey	cream

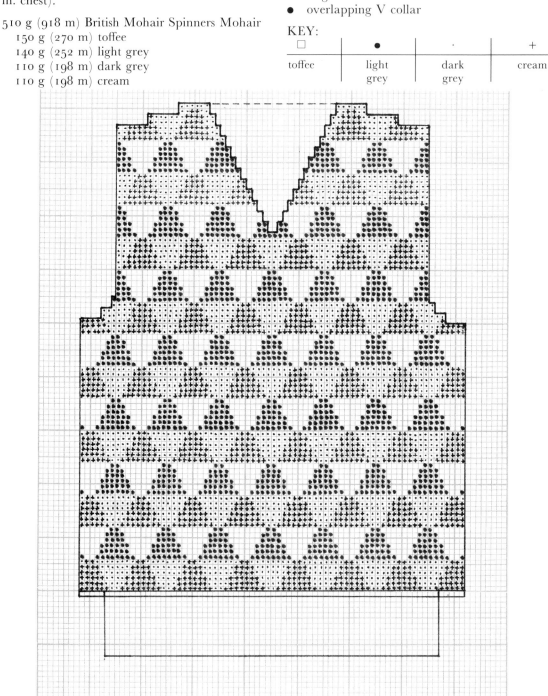

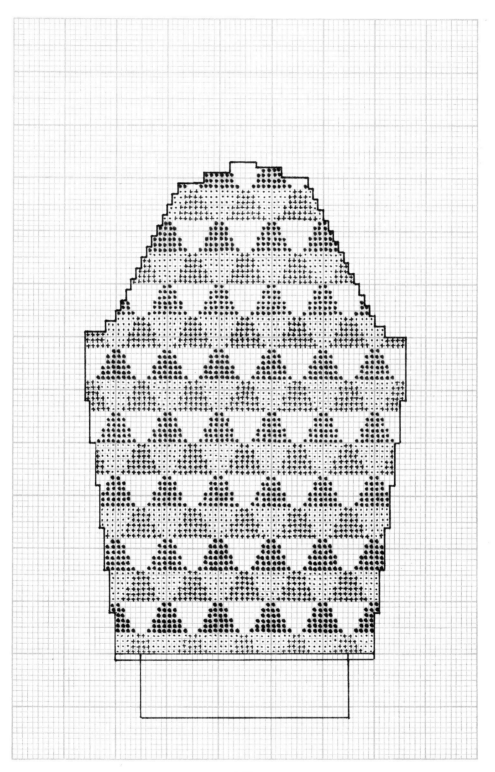

'DIAMONDS'

See colour plate 3. (Example fits 92–97 cm/36–38 in. chest.)

325 g (650 m) Listers '5 Star' Mohair
125 g Listers 'Bamboo' 100% cotton *or* contrast colour mohair
420 wooden beads

- **V-neck pattern**
- shaped sleeve
- overlapping V collar
- single rib cuffs and welt
- beaded knitting (method 1)

KEY:

background = mohair

□		●
main colour yarn	cotton yarn or contrast colour	bead

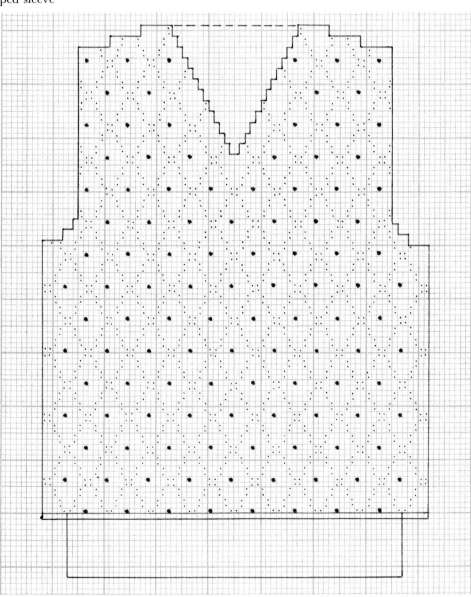

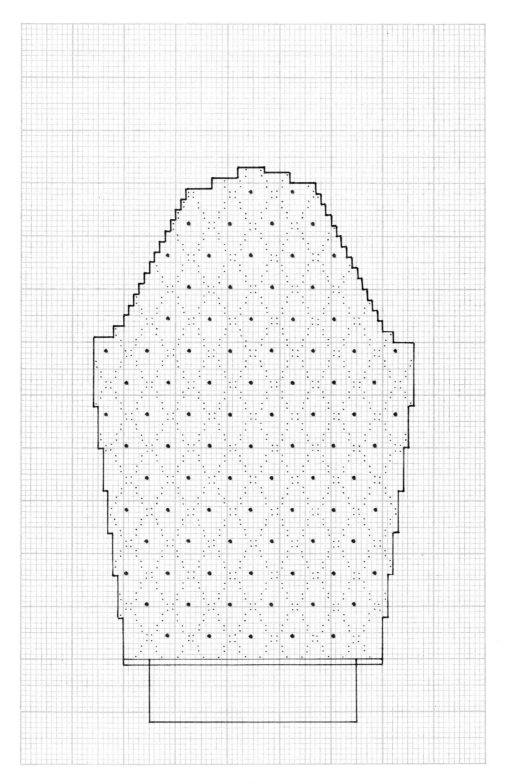

'VIKING'

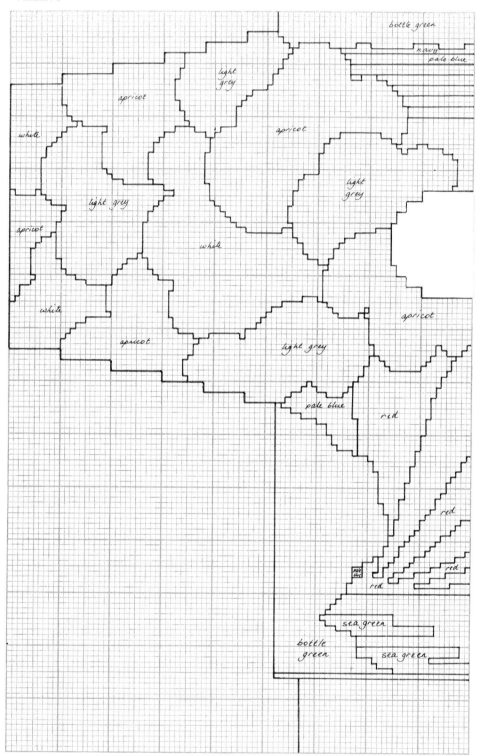

Continued on page 148–9

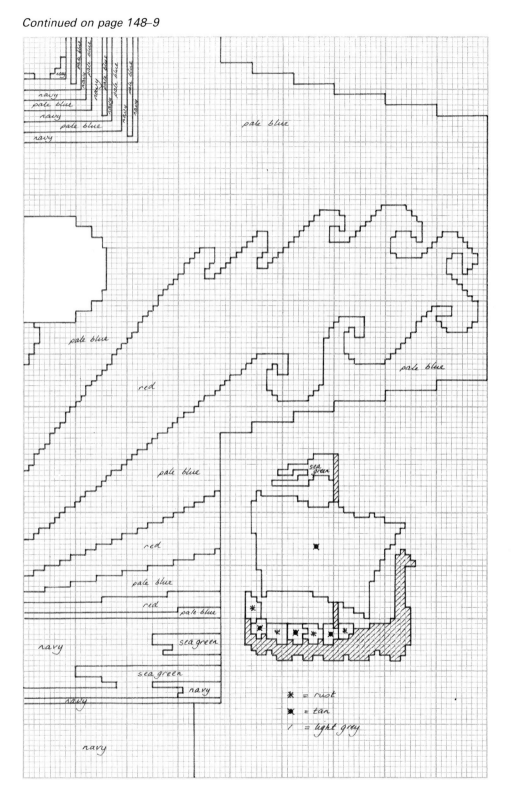

navy
pale blue
navy
pale blue
navy

pale blue

pale blue

red

pale blue

pale blue

red

pale blue

red

pale blue

sea green

sea green

navy

navy

navy

sea
green

* = rust
* = tan
/ = light grey

147

'VIKING'

See colour plate 8. (Example fits 66–71 cm/26–28 in. chest.)

325 g (650 m) Jonelle Mohair
   75 g (150 m) pale blue
   50 g (100 m) navy
   50 g (100 m) bottle green
   50 g (100 m) red
   25 g (50 m) white
   25 g (50 m) apricot
   25 g (50 m) sea green
   25 g (50 m) light grey
small amounts of rust and tan

- **dolman pattern**
- polo neck collar edged in contrast colour
- single rib cuffs grafted on to sleeves
- single rib welt
- Swiss darning for ship
- embroidered sheep's faces and legs
- bobbles for sheep's bodies
- separate balls of yarn for isolated shapes

KEY:

pb	n	··	sg	▨	*	✖	●
pale blue	navy	white	sea green	light grey	rust	tan	bobble

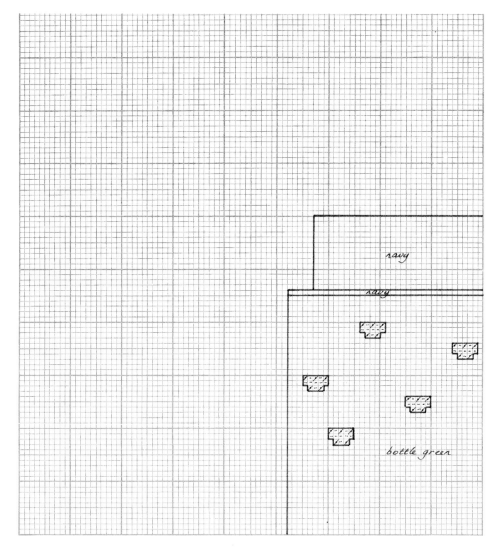

148

149

'SNOWFLAKE'

See colour plate 9. (Example fits 82–87 cm/32–34 in. chest.)

525 g (1050 m) Jonelle Mohair
   275 g (550 m) white
   100 g (200 m) bright blue
   75 g (150 m) red
   50 g (100 m) bottle green
   25 g (50 m) yellow

- **raglan pattern**
- raglan sleeve
- cowl collared hood
- single rib cuffs and welt

KEY:

□	●	×	✹	·
white	bright blue	red	bottle green	yellow

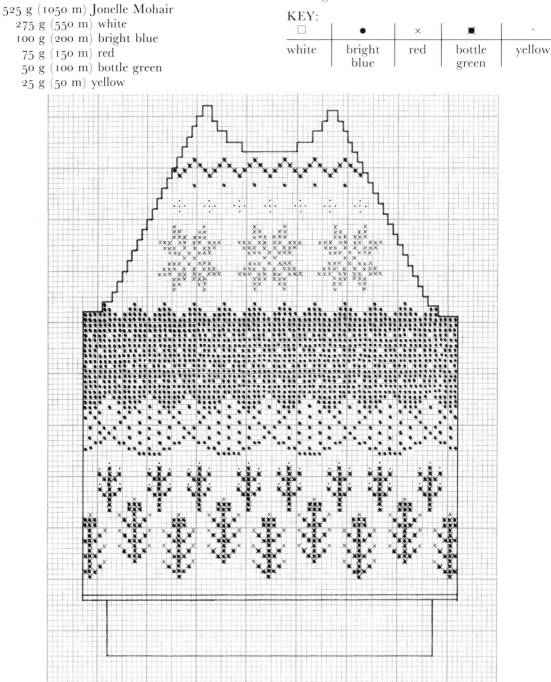

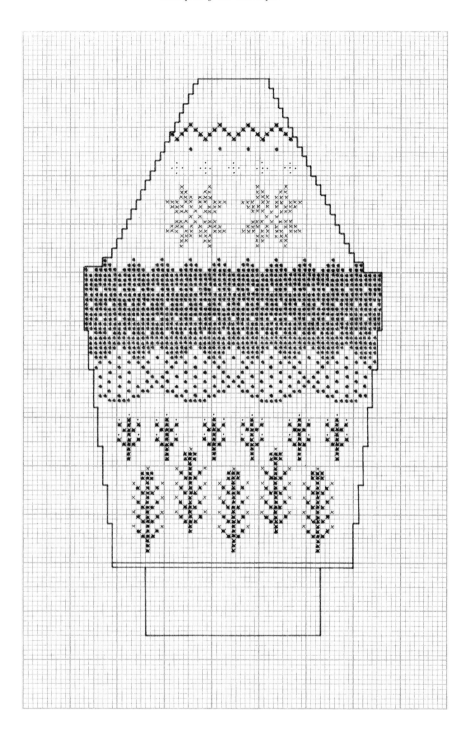

'EAGLE'

See colour plate 10. (Example fits 82–87 cm/32–34 in. chest.)

360 g (720 m) Jonelle Mohair
   225 g (450 m) black
   135 g (270 m) white

- **raglan pattern**
- swollen garter stitch collar
- single rib cuffs and welt

152

KEY:

●	□
black	white

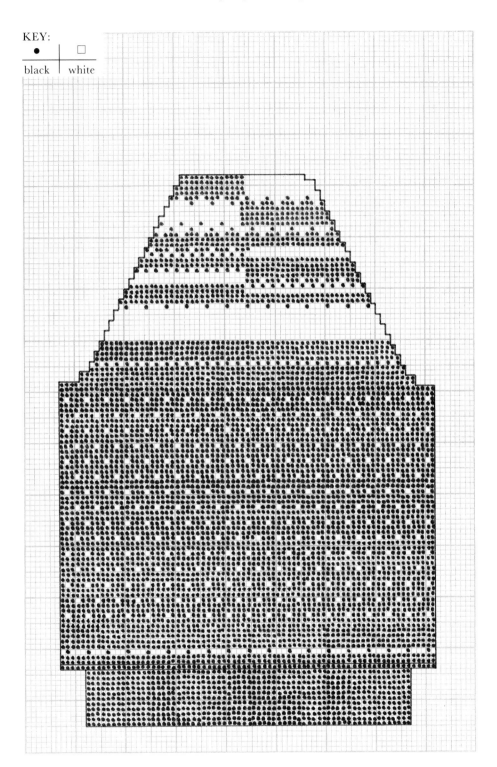

'MOONLIGHT'

See colour plate 12. (Example fits 87–92 cm/34–36 in. chest.)

KEY:

dg/●	/	□	○	·	×
dark grey	light grey	beige	silver lurex	pink lurex	bobbles on the back only

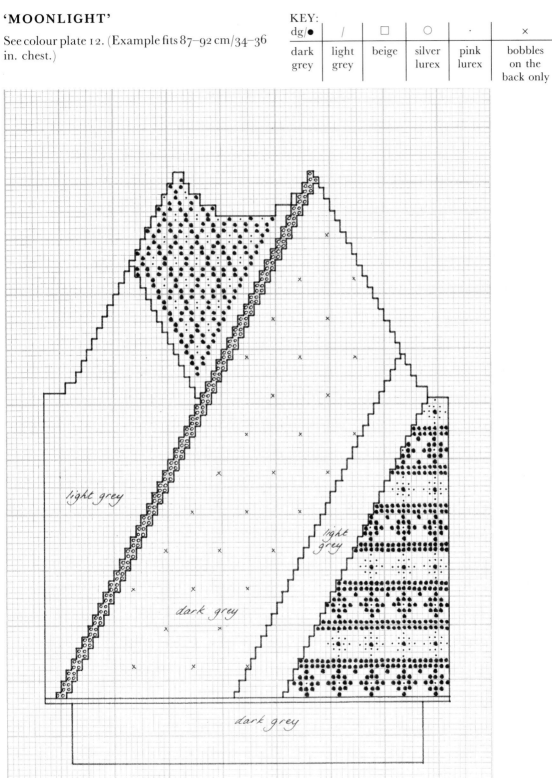

light grey

dark grey

light grey

dark grey

dark grey

360 g (648 m) British Mohair Spinners Mohair
    180 g (324 m) dark grey
    140 g (252 m) light grey
    40 g (72 m) beige
    25 g silver Lurex thread
    25 g pink Lurex thread

- **raglan pattern**
- raglan sleeve
- overlay slit collar, cast on edge and side edges in Lurex
- single rib cuffs and welt
- bobbles on the back

KEY:

dg/●	/	□	○	·	×
dark grey	light grey	beige	silver lurex	pink lurex	bobbles on the back only

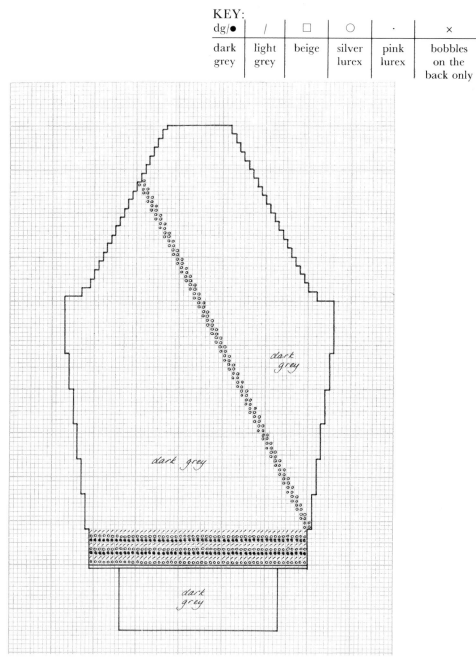

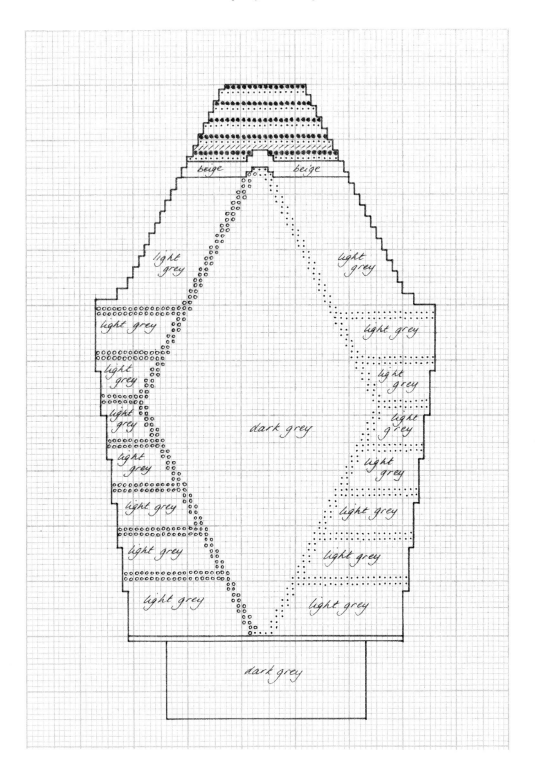

'MIDNIGHT'

See colour plate 14. (Example fits 97–102 cm/38–40 in. chest.)

950g (1900 m) Jonelle Mohair
   725 g (1450 m) navy
   100 g (200 m) black
   75 g (150 m) bright blue
   50 g (100 m) white

- **reversible one-piece jacket pattern**
- full sleeves
- swollen rib collar
- single rib cuffs and welt
- vertical Y-shaped button bands
- vertical slit pocket on plain side
- Fair Isle pattern on reverse side
- Pearl beads sewn in centre of diamonds before making up

KEY (to chart on this page):

●	/	.	□
navy	bright blue	white	black

'STAINED GLASS'

See colour plate 13. (Example fits 87–92 cm/34–36 in. chest.)

700 g (1400 m) Jonelle Mohair
   550 g (1100 m) grey
   75 g (100 m) sage green
   50 g (100 m) black
   25 g (50 m) white
20 buttons
pearl beads

- **reversible one-piece jacket pattern**
- armbands
- swollen rib collar
- single rib cuffs and welt
- vertical slit pocket on plain side
- Fair Isle pattern on reverse side
- pearl beads sewn in centre of diamonds before making up

KEY (to chart on this page):
background = light grey

●	/	.	□
light grey	black	white	sage green

158

'SORAYA'

See colour plate 14. (Example fits 92–97 cm/36–38 in.)

350 g (700 m) Jonelle Mohair
75 cm of 112 cm wide material
10 buttons.

- **reversible one-piece jacket pattern**
- armbands.
- swollen rib collar
- single rib cuffs and welt
- vertical Y-shaped button bands
- vertical slit pocket
- lined with material
- welt edging

ABBREVIATIONS

alt	alternate		**psso**	pass the slip stitch over
beg	beginning		**rem**	remaining
cm	centimetre		**rep**	repeat
cont	continue		**rev st st**	reverse stocking stitch
cross 2R	cross 2 stitches to the right		**sl**	slip
cross 2L	cross 2 stitches to the left		**st(s)**	stitch(es)
dec	decrease		**st st**	stocking stitch
dc	double crochet		**tbl**	through the back of the loop
foll	following		**tog**	together
g	gram		**tr**	treble crochet
inc	increase		**turn**	turn the work and continue to pattern back along the row from this point
in.	inches			
k	knit		**y bk**	yarn back
k2 tog	knit 2 together		**y fwd**	yarn forward
m 1	make one		**yrn**	yarn round the needle
no	number		*** ***	when a pattern is written between asterisks, e.g., *k1, p3, k2 tog, p3*, the pattern is repeated as many times as possible along the row
p	purl			
patt	pattern			

Conversion Tables

KNITTING NEEDLE CONVERSION CHART

Continental (mm)	British	US
2.25	13	0
2.75	12	1
3	11	2
3.25	10	3
3.75	9	4
4	8	5
4.5	7	6
5	6	7
5.5	5	8
6	4	9
6.5	3	10
7	2	10.5
7.5	1	11
8.5	00	13
9	000	15

METRIC/IMPERIAL CONVERSION CHART

Please note that these conversions are *approximate* to the nearest quarter inch.

cm	in.
1	$\frac{1}{2}$
2	$\frac{3}{4}$
3	$1\frac{1}{4}$
4	$1\frac{1}{2}$

cm	in.
5	2
6	$2\frac{1}{4}$
7	$2\frac{3}{4}$
8	$3\frac{1}{4}$
9	$3\frac{1}{2}$
10	4
11	$4\frac{1}{4}$
12	$4\frac{3}{4}$
13	5
14	$5\frac{1}{2}$
15	6
16	$6\frac{1}{4}$
17	$6\frac{3}{4}$
18	7
19	$7\frac{1}{2}$
20	$7\frac{3}{4}$
21	$8\frac{1}{4}$
22	$8\frac{3}{4}$
23	9
24	$9\frac{1}{2}$
25	$9\frac{3}{4}$
26	$10\frac{1}{4}$
27	$10\frac{3}{4}$
28	11
29	$11\frac{1}{2}$
30	$11\frac{3}{4}$
31	$12\frac{1}{4}$
32	$12\frac{1}{2}$
33	13
34	$13\frac{1}{2}$
35	$13\frac{3}{4}$
36	$14\frac{1}{4}$

cm	in.
37	$14\frac{1}{2}$
38	15
39	$15\frac{1}{4}$
40	$15\frac{3}{4}$
41	16
42	$16\frac{1}{2}$
43	17
44	$17\frac{1}{4}$
45	$17\frac{3}{4}$
46	18
47	$18\frac{1}{2}$
48	19
49	$19\frac{1}{4}$
50	$19\frac{3}{4}$
51	20
52	$20\frac{1}{2}$
53	$20\frac{3}{4}$
54	$21\frac{1}{4}$
55	$21\frac{3}{4}$
56	22
57	$22\frac{1}{2}$
58	$22\frac{3}{4}$
59	$23\frac{1}{4}$
60	$23\frac{1}{2}$

GRAM/OUNCE CONVERSION CHART

Please note that these conversions are *approximate* to the nearest quarter ounce. One ounce = approximately 28.35 grams.

grams	ounces
25	1
50	$1\frac{1}{4}$
75	$2\frac{3}{4}$
100	$3\frac{1}{2}$
125	$4\frac{1}{2}$
150	$5\frac{1}{4}$
175	$6\frac{1}{4}$
200	7
225	8
250	$8\frac{3}{4}$
275	$9\frac{3}{4}$
300	$10\frac{1}{2}$
325	$11\frac{1}{2}$
350	$12\frac{1}{4}$
375	$13\frac{1}{4}$
400	14
425	15
450	$15\frac{3}{4}$
475	$16\frac{1}{2}$
500	$17\frac{1}{2}$

SUPPLIERS

OF YARNS CONTAINING MOHAIR

UNITED KINGDOM

Argyll Wools Ltd
10 St George St
off Conduit St
London W1R 9DF

British Mohair Spinners
Grove Mills
Ingrow
Keighley
West Yorkshire

Emu International Ltd
Leeds Road
Idle
Bradford BD10 9TE

Filatura di Crosa
Priory Yarns Ltd
24 Prospect Road
Osset
West Yorkshire WF5 8AE

Hayfield Textiles Ltd
Hayfield Mills
Glusburn
Keighley BD20 8QP

Jaeger Hand Knitting Ltd
PO Box
McMullen Rd
Darlington DL1 1YH

Jonelle
John Lewis Partnership
Metford House
15–18 Clipstone St
London W1A 2LT

Lister-Lee
George Lee and Sons Ltd
Whiteoak Mills
Wakefield
West Yorkshire WF2 9SF

Patons & Baldwins Ltd
McMullen Rd
Darlington DL1 1YQ

Georges Picaud
Priory Yarns
24 Prospect Road
Osset
West Yorkshire WF5 8AE

Pingouin Wools
7–11 Lexington St
London W1R 4BU

Robin Wools Ltd
Robin Mills Ltd
Idle
Bradford BD10 9TE

Patricia Roberts
60 Kinnerton St
London SW1

Sirdar PLC
PO Box 31
Averthorpe
Wakefield WF2 9ND

3 Suisses
Filatures de l'Espierres
Marlborough House
38 Welford Rd
Leicester LE2 7AA

Wendy
Carter and Parker Ltd
Guisely
West Yorkshire LS20 9PD

Also useful:
Creative Beadcraft Ltd
Unit 26
Chiltern Trading Estate
Earl Howe Road
Holmer Green
High Wycombe
Buckinghamshire
Supply beads suitable for knitwear.

International Mohair Association
28 Albermarle Street
London W1X 3FA
Tel: 01–409 1431
Can provide information on availability of yarns and patterns.

US

Bernat Yarn & Craft Corp.
Depot & Mendon Sts
Uxbridge
MA 01569

Anny Blatt
24770 Crestview Ct
Farmington
MI 48018

Gemini Innovations Ltd
720 East Jericho Tpke
Huntingdon Station
NY 11746

Jaeger
Susan Bates
Rte 9A
Chester
CT 06412

Lion Brand Yarns
524 W.23rd St
New York
NY 10011

Patons
Susan Bates
Rte 9A
Chester
CT 06412

Phildar Inc
6438 Dawson Blvd
Norcross
GA 30093

Georges Picaud
Merino Yarn Co
230 5th Ave
New York
NY 10001

Pingouin
PO Box 100
Highway 45
Jamestown
SC 29453

Schaffhauser Wool
3489 NW Yeon
Portland
OR 97210

Scheepjeswool Inc
155 Lafayette Ave
N White Plains
NY 10603

Tahki Yarns
92 Kennedy St
Hackensack
NJ 07601

Welcomme
Mark Distributors Inc
PO Box 833
Chatsworth
CA 91311

Also useful:
Ms Maddy Daddiego
Mohair Council of America
1412 Broadway
New York 1001F

CANADA

Bernat Yarns Ltd
48 Milner Ave.
Scarborough, Ont.
M1S 3P8

Anny Blatt
Diamond Yarns Inc.
6797 St Laurence Blvd
Montreal PQ
H3L 2N1

Brunswick
SR Kertzer Ltd
257 Adelaide St West
Toronto, Ont.
M5H 1Y1

Patons & Baldwins (Canada) Inc.
Susan Bates
1001 Roselawn Ave.
Toronto, Ont.
M6B 1BS

Pingouin Yarns
Promafil Canada Ltee
1500 Rue Jules-Poitras
St Laurent, PQ
H4N 1X7

Schaffhauser
White Knitting Products
1470 Birchmount Rd
Scarborough, Ont.
M1P 2G1

Scheepjeswool (Canada) Ltd
400 B Montee de Liesse
Montreal, PQ
H4T 1NS

3 Suisses
Diamond Yarn (Canada) Corp.
9697 St Laurent Blvd
Montreal, PQ
H3L 2N1

Tahki
Gerald H. Whitaker Ltd
12 Keefer Rd
St Catharines, Ont.
L2M 7N9

Welcomme
Craftsmen Distributors Inc.
4166 Halifax St
Burnaby, BC
V5C 3X2

INDEX